SYKES IN ERITREA

SYKES IN ERITREA

Photography
Lawrence F. Sykes

in reflection

Poetry
Charles Cantalupo

THE RED SEA PRESS

Trenton | London | New Delhi | Cape Town | Nairobi | Addis Ababa | Asmara | Ieadan

THE RED SEA PRESS
541 West Ingham Avenue | Suite B
Trenton, New Jersey 08638

Book design: Dawid Kahts
Cover design: Dawid Kahts

Cataloging-in-Publication Data may be obtained from the Library of Congress.

ISBN: 9781569028117 $84.95 HB
        978156908124 $24.95 . PB

Contents

Sykes in Eritrea   1

On the World   55

List of Images   96

Acknowledgements   97

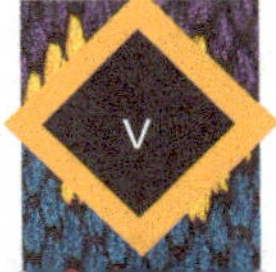

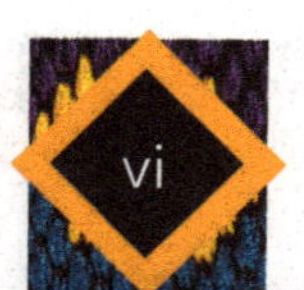

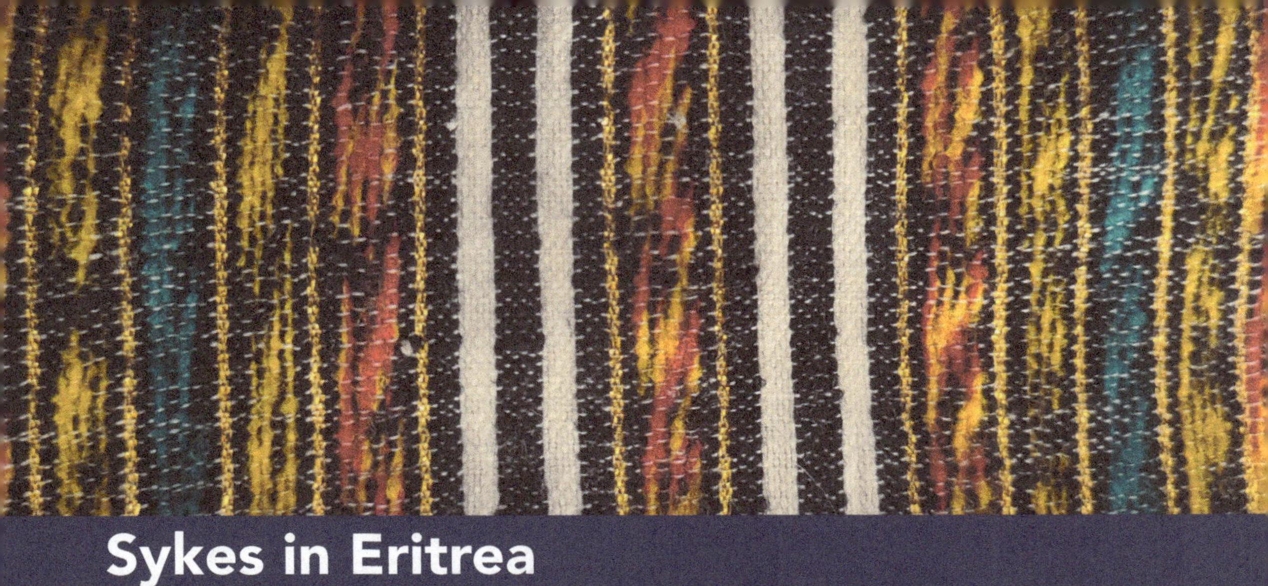

Sykes in Eritrea

Lawrence F. Sykes, born in Alabama, 1931:
Son of the dentist, Frank J. Sykes, and the teacher, Alice West;
Grandson of Solomon Sharper Sykes, born into slavery,
Who became the "well-known local Negro undertaker" and
"Who had won for himself by his acts of kindness many friends,"
In the words of *The Decatur Daily*'s obituary,
May 1925, where the record of Sykes family
Roots runs so deep and can wander in so many directions
That when I read about them, I see why Eritrea would
Pull Larry in when I told my friend and mentor about it
In 1995 when I first went there, and he went, too,
In '98 and 2000. Larry Sykes identified
With a place to the point that it all but seemed like he was home
Through a spontaneous kind of visual tapping into
Places with histories strewn across their surfaces set deep
In counter histories: layers of the broken and intact
Constantly moving among each other; one moment settling
And the next jostling in Haiti, Europe, India, Brazil
Cuba, America, Africa. Yet he once said to me,
"I take the picture I don't see till it happens," and with that
We started working together. Ngũgĩ wa Thiong'o was
Living in Orange, New Jersey. I would ask him questions, and
Larry would photograph him. The plan seemed straightforward enough:
Interview published with pictures of the great Kenyan writer.
This seemed like plenty in January 1993,
When it took place, but in Orange I was also going back:
Born and raised five minutes from where Ngũgĩ now lived in exile,
And where I'd buy the same bread at the Italian bakery

After the interview that my family bought for decades.
This felt incongruous, and I told Sykes, which he said he liked.
Little did know I know how much as we both shared some of the bread.

Sykes lived in Boston's Jamaica Plain and drove down in his Saab.
Living in Bethlehem PA in the historic district,
I had invited him to stay at my house the night before.
We'd drive together to Orange, which would take around an hour.
I'd heard of Larry through editing a book on Ngũgĩ.
It would be called *The World of Ngũgĩ wa Thiong'o*, and
Frank Chipasula was in it, a Malawian writer.
"Singing Like Parrots," his poem on the Kenyan dictator
Who had imprisoned Ngũgĩ, would be perfect for the book.
When I phoned Frank for permission, he said "yes" and offered names
Of other scholars on Ngũgĩ. Larry hadn't worked on him.
But Sykes had helped Chipasula who was also in exile.
"Try Larry Sykes" was part quid pro quo but Frank also said this:
"Look up his visual work on Michael Harper, the poet,
And for a conference in Washington DC on Sterling Brown."
Seeing these images for the first time, I wanted Larry
To be a part of the Ngũgĩ book, beginning with pictures
During the interview. So, I called and told him my idea,
Leading to opening my front door at 10 PM one night
And my first meeting the six foot eight Sykes standing, loaded down
Not only with his photography equipment and small bag
To stay the night but with bottles of shiraz and two pounds of
Yirgacheffe coffee beans; both would turbocharge our next day's plans.

Next morning and driving east on interstate 78,
We talked nonstop almost randomly of art and politics.
Larry squeezed into the front seat of my small Eagle Talon.
As I sped over the Delaware and eased into fifth gear,
Sykes started talking about himself but by the fourth sentence
"Born in Decatur…" and his birth, 9/10/1931
Changed to what happened in Alabama sixty-five miles east:
Scottsboro, six months before; 3/25 to be exact.
Riding a freight train two women who were white claim they'd been raped
By nine black teenagers. Only one, the youngest, age thirteen
Wasn't convicted and as was common in Alabama
Sentenced to death: which took barely two weeks and without any
Medical evidence that a rape took place. Still the belief
That a black man always raped white women if he got the chance
Ran up and down the hills of this otherwise pastoral place.

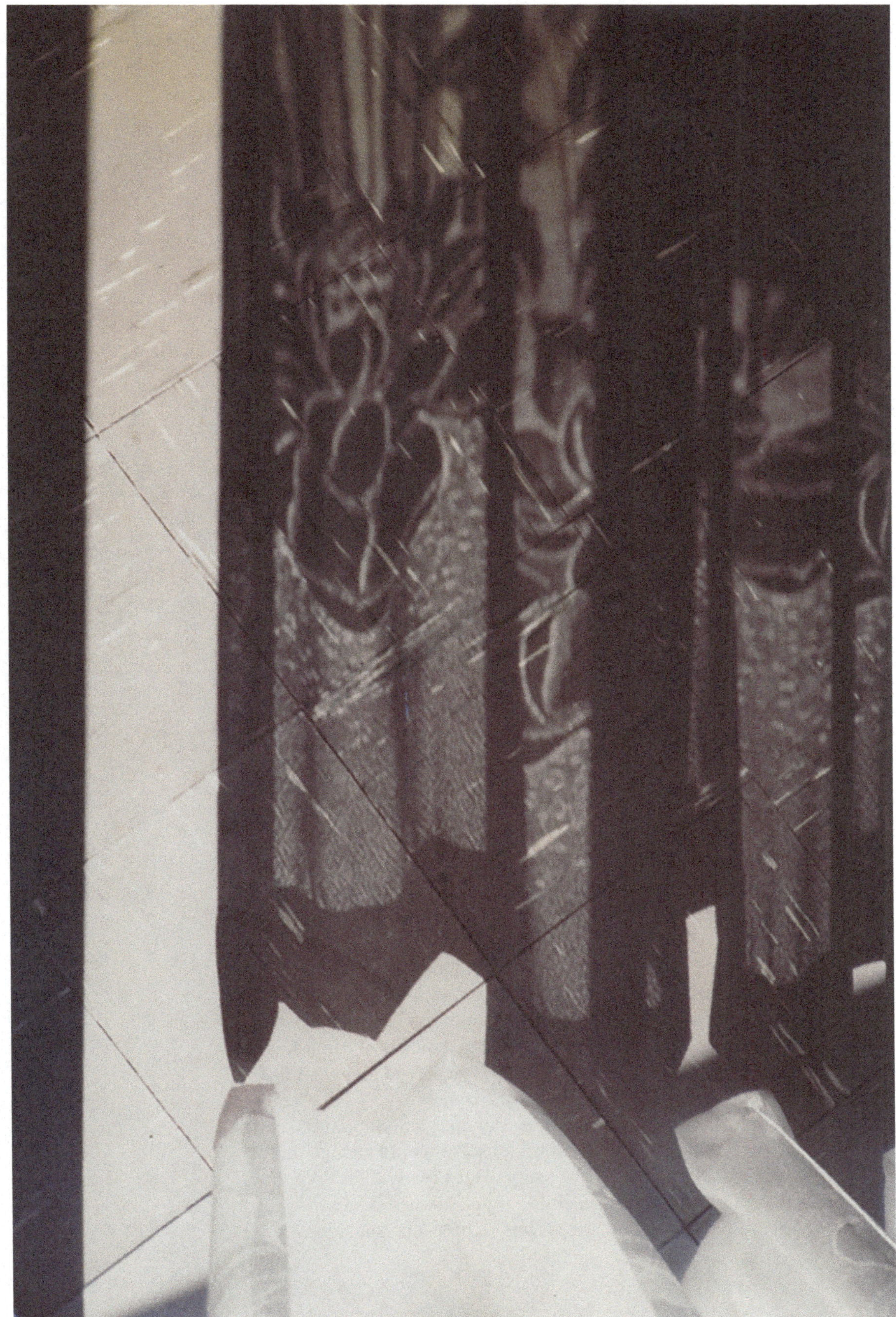

After appeals and a ruling by the US Supreme Court
That overturned the conviction, in March 1933,
New trials took place, but a change of venue also was ordered:
Morgan, a neighboring county, and in rural Decatur,
Where the Sykes family – Solomon and his three brothers, too –
Thrived in the era of black emancipation: in business,
Politics, medicine, education, and development
Of the community, so that they were highly respected.
Solomon's death, therefore, prompted Larry's father in his move
Back to Decatur to oversee the family fortune
And build his own, newly married, as he started to practice
Dentistry in his hometown in 1926; eight years
After he got his degree from Howard in 1918.
As in the Scottsboro trial, Decatur spawned its own lynch mobs
Frequently gathered outside the jail and threatened the young men.
Doctor Sykes worked with the sheriff, moving them to a safe place.
As did the northern reporters, targeted for their stories,
Need to be safeguarded from the local outpouring of hate.
Nor did the vitriol and the death threats spare Larry's father.

One night a KKK cross burned on the Bank Street property
Owned by Sykes and right outside the building where the family
Funeral home was and where he had his dental office, too.
More KKK crosses in Decatur meant the time had come
For Frank to move again: late in '37 and once more
Open a practice in Baltimore, where he found an office
Over a bar near Johns Hopkins University hospital.
In the surrounding black, busy neighborhood filled with orderlies
And other hospital workers, Larry lived and went to school;
Nearby row houses of Slavic women mopping their doorsteps
And the street, too: enough sanctuary for the Sykes children,
So that their fate wouldn't be the same as the Scottsboro Boys.

Larry paused or did he end his story? I asked a question,
Trying to keep my eyes on the road and look at him also.
"Now what does Scottsboro make you think?" His answer surprised me,
And he laughed at first, "That's not a question you can ask Ngũgĩ.
But I can say the oppression was so widespread and went on,
On and on in early 30s Alabama, the trial
And the convictions gone all the way up to the Supreme Court
Only to be reversed, and sent back as if it would change things
Swirling with more and more fury. But I really didn't see
Any of that back then as a child.   I just learned it later.
I could see only my loving parents. There's no substitute

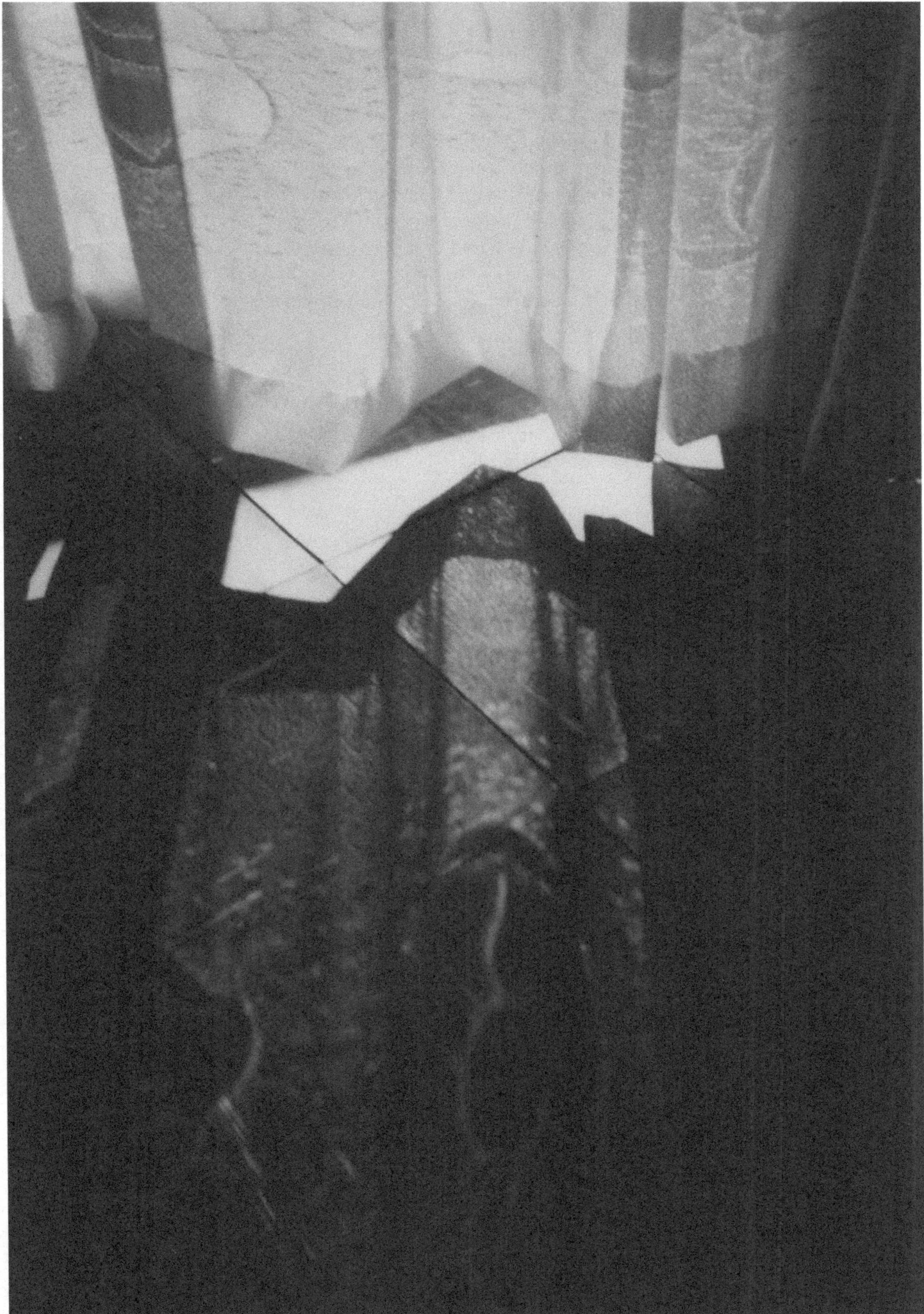

For the start that they can give you: images and the feeling
Carried until your last day." Thus, Larry's love for history
And counter history that came out in what he created
Still had this sine qua non from Alice and his father, Frank:
History was Sykes own heartbeat first and then the heartbeat of
History that he saw deeply rooted in the everyday
Images that he found all around the world to feel like home.

History haunted me when I went with him to my hometown
Planning incongruously to interview Africa's great
Writer who lived there now. But my history only went back
To Ellis Island, east twenty miles of Orange, New Jersey,
And a ship's manifest listing my grandfather's name, Carlo,
Ninety-nine years before, when he landed from Calabria.
What in my family came before that I have no idea.

That's not the case with Sykes. *Early Settlers of Alabama*,
James Edmunds Saunders' book, which was published 1899,
Covers the family of Sykes, though not all of it for sure.
Dr. Frank W. Sykes, born 1819, was Saunders'
"Neighbor" for "forty years" and "I…never had a better one,"
Saunders writes, praising the man's accomplishments and character
As a physician, a politician, plantation owner:
Family man who was "honest and efficient" yet a mind
"[O]f…robust order…an earnest…forcible debater" and
"[A]lways respected." The *New York Times* called him "a Union man
During the war," and Sykes was "fairly elected," writes Saunders,
As US senator during Reconstruction, "but he was"
In 1872 "unjustly" not allowed his seat.
Yet before that "[h]e was several times elected to the House"
In Alabama and served in the state senate subsequent
To Lee's surrender and downfall of the Confederacy.
Why the successful physician entered politics could be
Traced to his marrying into a political family.
His wife, Elizabeth, was the daughter of the general and
Longstanding senator, Jesse Garth, who lived near Decatur.
Saunders says he was "a man of note and influence," so he
Would have been wealthy and owned slaves, too, in the1840s.
Dr. Frank W. Sykes, according to current research
By the Sykes family, got a wedding gift: a young black slave
Who was named Laura. Elizabeth and he had five children.
Laura and he had six, one of whom would be Solomon Sykes,
Not only Larry's grandfather but his great grandfather's slave.

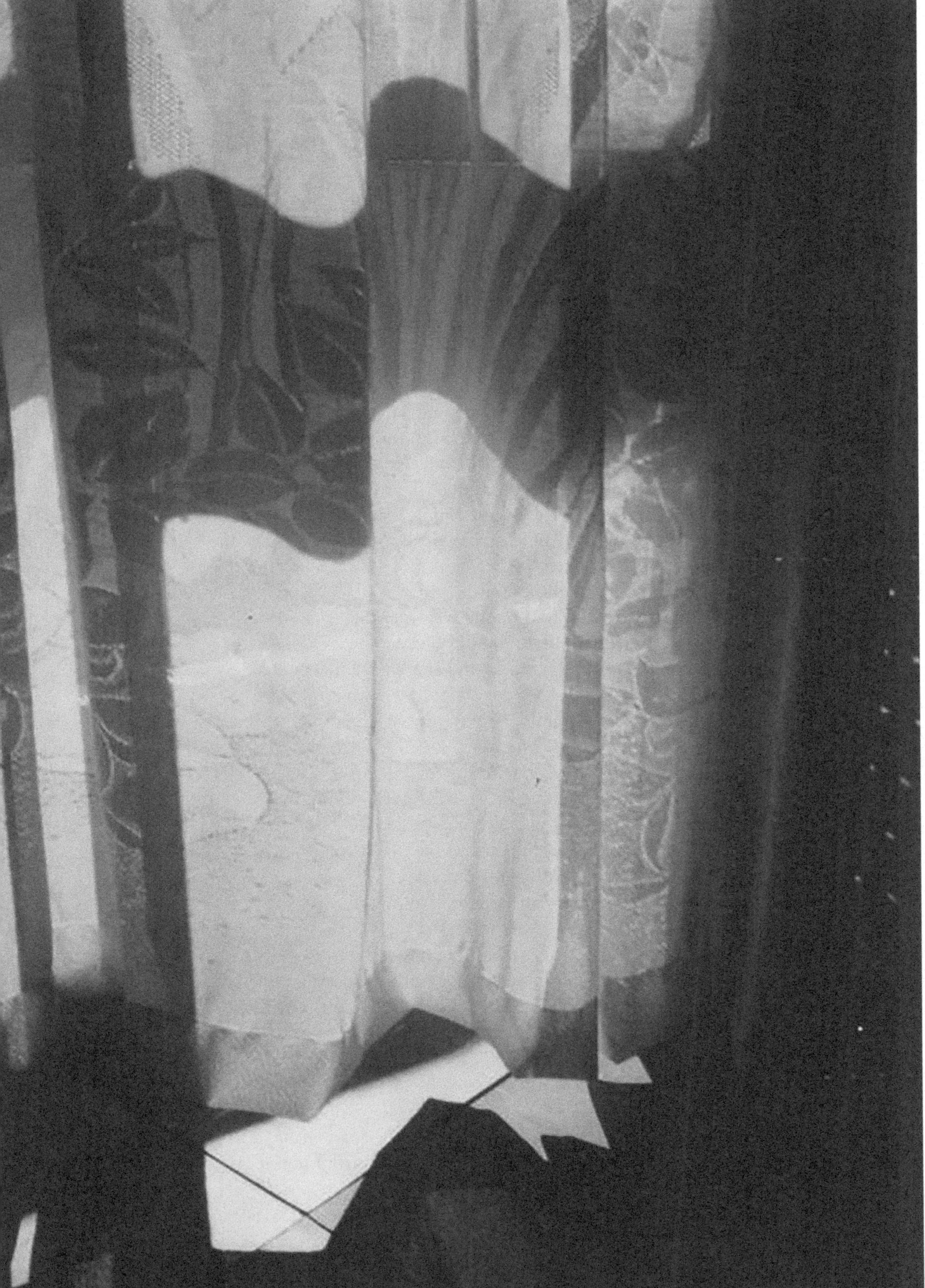

Whether the history my grandfather left in Italy
Is anything like this, I may never know, but when I told
Larry the story of how I felt going back to Orange
He slowly said my last name and paused at every syllable.
Then he laughed, "I knew that you were up to something when you called."
Maybe I was but from that point on and for twenty-five years
Sykes always guided me on the path I couldn't see alone.
As did his father decide to leave behind like my grandpa
One kind of history burning so another kind could be.

From 1914 to 1924, Larry's father,
Living in Baltimore and at Howard getting his degree
Prior to his move back home and dentistry in Decatur,
Went by the name "Doc Sykes" and pitched in the Negro baseball league.
This must have fed Larry's liking sports, too. He played basketball.
Black students still went to segregated schools in Baltimore.
So, he excelled at Paul Laurence Dunbar High School. The "big man"
Also starred at the historically black college, Morgan State.
Long Island U was the next step on the ladder of sports fame.
Basketball playing days ended there in 1954.
Injuries at backup center sent him back to Morgan State
For a BA in Arts Education, although not before
Barbara Swann met him in New York, and she would marry him.
Larry came back for an Arts MA from Pratt, and Barbara taught.
Larry would teach, too: first in the New York City schools then back
At Morgan State. When Rhode Island College in '67
Offered a visual arts position, Larry accepted.
Moving to Providence, he became Professor Sykes, revered
Both as a teacher and artist who inspired his students.
Many of them became artists, too, because they followed him.
In 1995, Sykes retired. His making art increased.
Who was he? I can remember Barbara once telling me
Only half joking and lovingly: that "tall quiet black man
With short hair, wearing an overcoat, and taking a picture
Of himself in black and white reflected in a store window."
Barbara meant that he'd changed a lot since that first self-portrait,
And not the Sykes I would know and work with. He told a story.
"During the second world war a friend took me to a pawn shop,
And with the money that I had saved I bought a camera."

Larry with camera in the noontime January sun
Sharply reflecting off Ngũgĩ's ice and snow-covered front porch
Followed me up the steps. Njerri wa Ngũgĩ let us in,
Making us welcome with mango juice, Moroccan tangerines,

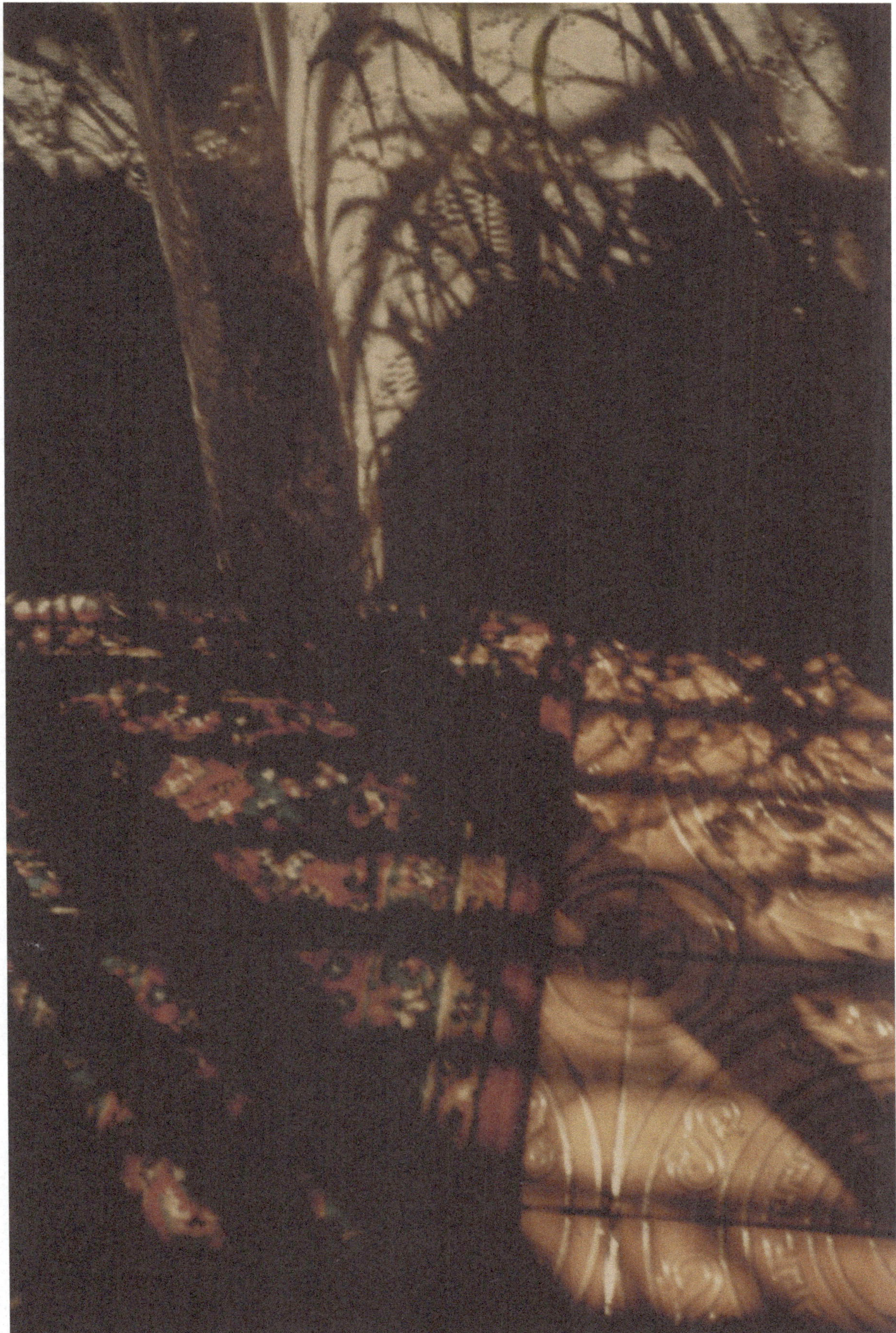

And reassurances that our conversation would go well
While she was making samosas and roast goat for our dinner.
Ngũgĩ' was late, coming home from New York, but in half an hour,
Hearing the back door slam, Njerri got us up from the table
And we were led to a sunny sitting room. Two banks of lights
Set up already by Larry, when I didn't know, pointed
Down at a large, curved, velour couch. Ngũgĩ' rushed in and we sat.
Sykes used his 35-millimeter Nikon for the shoot.
After three hours we all sensed it was enough, and Larry said,
"Other than you underneath these lights, there's something good cooking."
Smelling the goat roasting and unable to resist, we stopped.

Sykes sent me contact sheets two weeks later in an envelope
All but hermetically sealed with heavy padding thickly taped
(Over the years I'd get many more such packages from him).
Struggling to open it, I pulled out the pictures and was shocked:
Only expecting to find the rows and rows of Ngũgĩ's face.
What was I doing there? Larry shot the interview and sent
Head shots of both of us: sharp, clear, and reflective black and white;
As we responded to what each other said: not monologue –
Dialogue in the tilt of a head, a determined parting
Or a quick tightening of the lips, a smile, a furrowing
Brow, and the shadows around somebody's eyes closing to think.
Larry saw Africa's greatest writer exiled in Orange
And more than ever heard worldwide reconnecting with his home:
Writing not only in English but his native Gikuyu.
Sykes showed that I should be in that picture when I didn't know.
Merely the interview and a book were my expectation:
Not it beginning a dialogue with Ngũgĩ ever since;
Decades long and crossing continents to work together on
Conferences, manuscripts, publications, declarations, and
African languages in a literary renaissance.
Yet the same kinds of connections I would have with other great
African writers I still owe to that first shock of being
Lit and empowered by Sykes when he put me in the picture.

How Larry's contact sheets would affect me was incidental.
Out of his meeting with Ngũgĩ he created an opus
Nothing short of monumental. Merely chiaroscuro
Shots of the interview weren't enough for Sykes. He also made
Full-page collages: with painting, drawing, and other images
Mixed in with portraits of Ngũgĩ; details from his life and work.
Larry's five "conjurgraphs," as he called them, signaled something more
Would emerge from *The World of Ngũgĩ wa Thiong'o* than

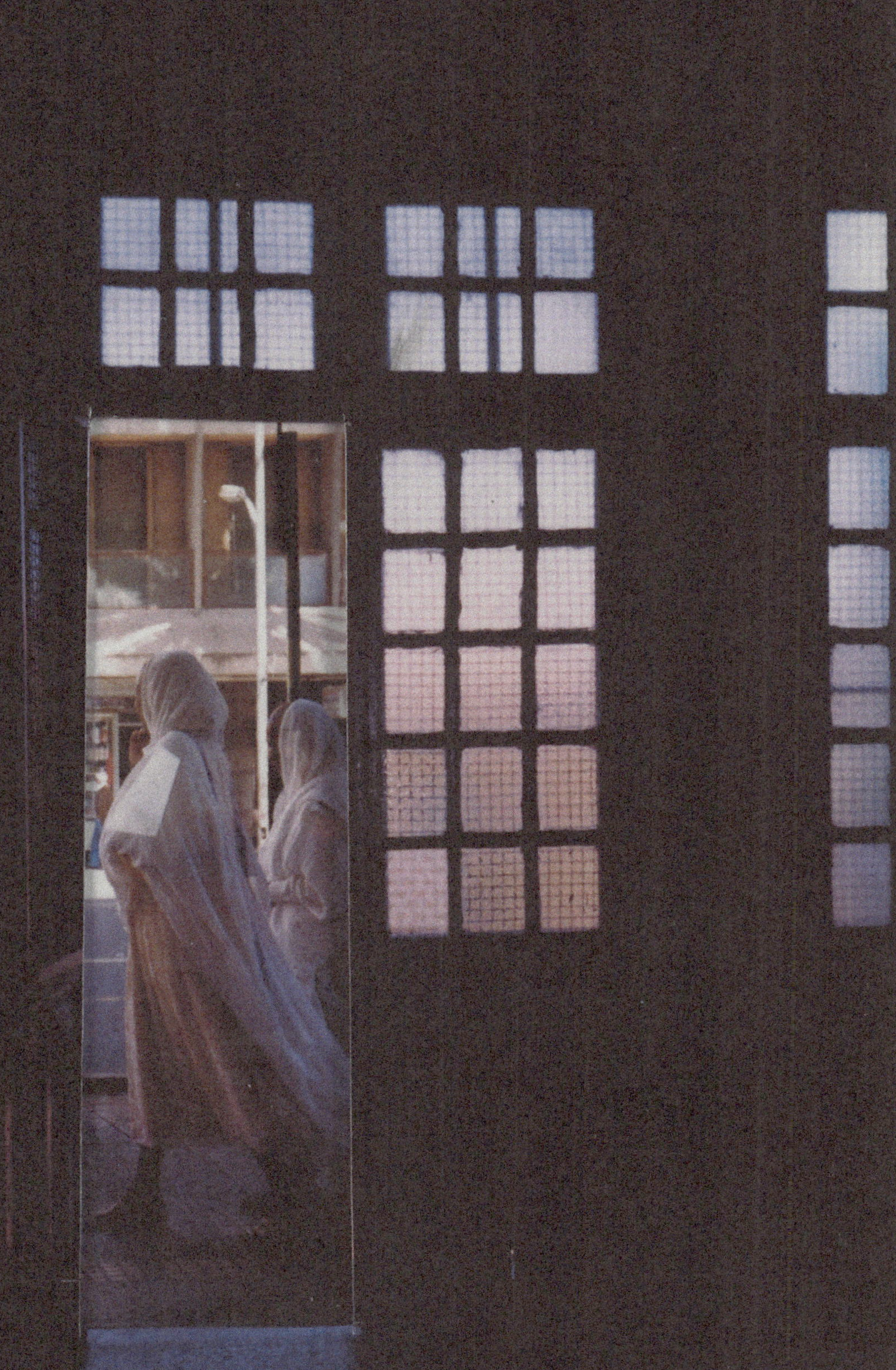

One little edited book I thought could be a good idea.

Not that my realizing Ngũgĩ's stature as a great writer
Wasn't belated and, frankly, ignorant – I will admit.
Talking with him and to see what Sykes made from the encounter
Led to my thinking a conference solely based on Ngũgĩ's work
Should take place, and I'd direct it. First I had to call Ngũgĩ'
For his permission. My second call was Sykes. Would he help me
And be advisor? We'd call it "Ngũgĩ wa Thiong'o," and
After a colon add "Text and Contexts." When Larry said "yes"
I knew it would be the largest on an African writer
Ever held in the US, the world, and even Africa.
Two hundred writers and scholars came from every continent.
Sykes as a consummate graphic artist offered an icon:
Fifteen connected and shaded spirals in a square diamond
Putting the conference name in Gikuyu first, then in English,
As they would be in the mind of Ngũgĩ, where his bright profile
Centered the image as innermost and diamond of diamonds
Etched in black on a rich, light brown background and firmly grounding
His face, the letters, and shaded spirals in concentric lines.
Larry's unique conference logo like his conjurgraphs once more
Typified his understanding of the Ngũgĩ narrative
Image to image and word to word and where he saw them join.
As did his picture become the cover of a second book
On Ngũgĩ's work and eponymously titled since it came
Out of the conference's presentations, also including
Poetry by Kamau Brathwaite, Sonia Sanchez, and from Newark –
Down from the Oranges and where Cantalupos made their home
When they first came to America – Amiri Baraka,
Whom I considered the greatest poet from where I grew up.
When I invited these poets, it was their intensity,
Though they had written on Ngũgĩ', which I most wanted to hear.
Yet the same word would apply to Larry since I first met him:
Still his intensity also felt like his understanding;
In the first night we talked, then how he described his growing up;
Shooting the interview, then the cover sheets; the conjurgraphs;
Pushing the conference idea and then the icon of Ngũgĩ'.
Nor did Sykes stop there. He made two conference art installations
Two Ngũgĩ monuments in a one-room gallery focused
First on "The Dictator," who forced Ngũgĩ to live in exile;
Next on the cultural bombs, as Ngũgĩ called them, exploding
Every day in what Sykes titled "The Colonial Classroom."
Talk about Larry's intensity, producing nothing less
Than a portfolio out of his engagement with Ngũgĩ.

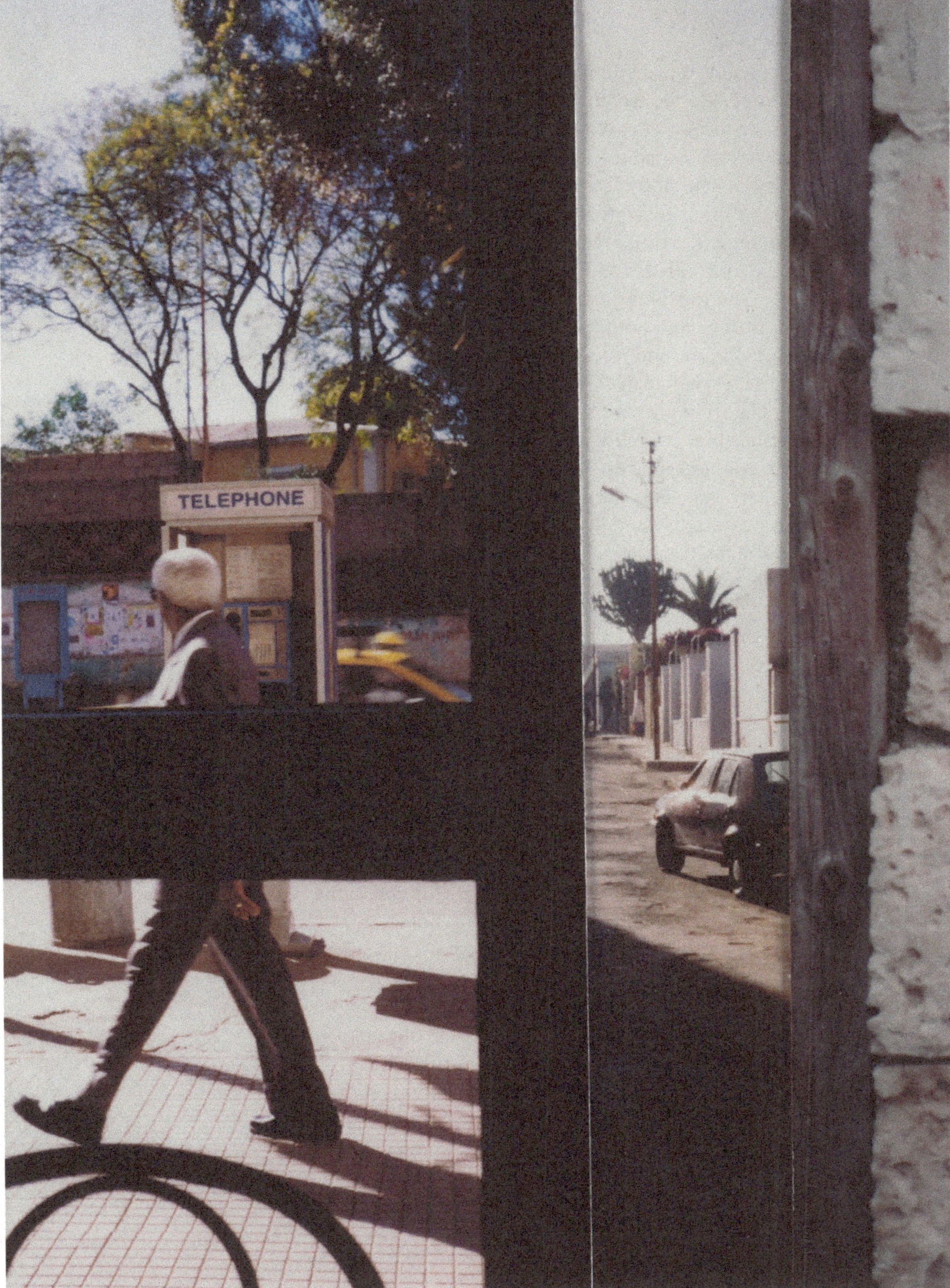
TELEPHONE

One of the conjurgraphs silhouettes a young man, hands on hips.
Posed contrapposto, he watches from a lush green riverbank
Water cascade through the Kenyan highlands, where he is alone.
British and French and some other flags from Europe drape the scene.
Ngũgĩ or some schoolboy like him has escaped there after school.
Sykes pastes a passage from Ngũgĩ's novel, *Devil on the Cross*.
We're to imagine the missionary's lacing into him.
"You must learn English and French or German, which are civilized
Languages. You must know names of mountains, rivers, lakes, and trees
That are in Europe and not first, like you say, your own country's
Animals, mountains, and rivers. When are you going to learn?"
Pasting the same passage in Gikuyu, the original
Written by Ngũgĩ before translating it into English,
Larry imagines him coping with the missionary's curse.
Not that the conjurgraph rests on that. Sykes seems to imagine
How the young man sees the missionary dead: his skeleton
On a scroll that might hang in a science classroom. Graffitied
Over the Latin and English names like "frontal bone," "sternum,"
"[J]aw," "metacarpal" are the Gikuyu names for the same bones.

Starker and sharper, a second conjurgraph Sykes created
Features a copy of the detention order for Ngũgĩ
In 1977 by the Kenyan government.
Dirty keys type out in Pica font the powers of the state
And "Regulations" that "satisfied" are "necessary for…
[P]ublic security to…control…by…restriction order"
Ngũgĩ's full name upper case and at the center of the page.
Next comes the actual "HEREBY ORDERS," also upper case,
And "that the…person shall be detained." It was the year's last day.
Underneath, Minister Daniel Arap Moi signs his full name
Largely and thickly and as if it might be indelible.
Not that Sykes let this official document remain unscathed,
Superimposing three graphic images on the order:
First like a postmark the seal of Kenya. Sykes always loved stamps,
And here he makes it look playful, as if it's not serious.
Far more imposingly, Larry focuses on Ngũgĩ's name;
Rather on where it took up the center of the document;
Blocking it with the detainee's profile, and as if he sees
Blue sky more clearly than ever, even if it's imagined,
Through the bars of his cell; and as he said in our interview,
Seeing "the seasons…of harvest…planting," and "of things growing"
All at once. Yet Sykes won't stop there, though I can't quite fathom this.
He has a large crow fly through the cell's bars. Yes, it's obvious,

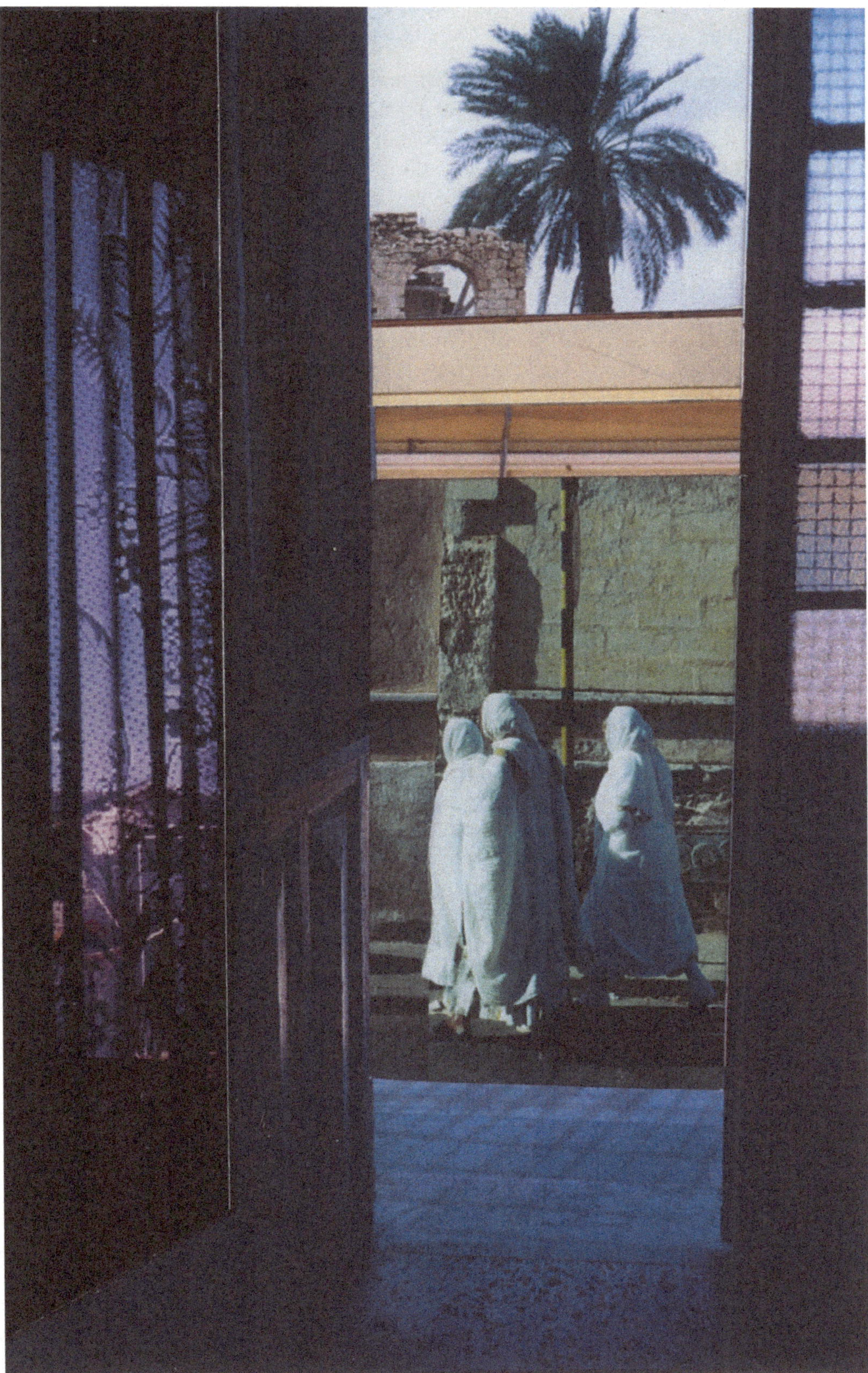

Meaning some kind of escape, however dark and difficult.
Or so I thought when I saw the image back in '93.
Nobody back then would realize, not Sykes, maybe not Ngũgĩ,
Such a crow more darkly stamped than anything else on the page
Would be a prophecy of the author's work ten years later:
His epic novel called *Wizard of the Crow*, and translated
From the Gikuyu, *Mũrogi wa Kagogo*, by Ngũgĩ.
How did Sykes know that *kagogo,* that big crow had to be there?

Larry collaged the same Ngũgĩ profile three more times but first
Free of the prison cell bars. The most elaborate pictures him
As if within a chart of the solar system and his head
Grazing the orbit of Mars. He seems to wear the orbits of
Mercury, Venus, and Earth like haloes. Thin bright pencil lines
Scribbled across his broad forehead shimmer with Mt. Kenya's snow
Looming behind him and with the gleaming limbs of the dancers
Drawn long ago in a cave now in the open down the slope:
Striking their poses of standing straight, stooped low and bending back;
Shoulders pulled up with their necks retracted and their arms waving.
Yet the same profile emerges from what seems like an ocean,
Only of tenement blocks and slums and Kenyan shantytowns.
Scribbling more lines on the dark, strong jaw Sykes reinforces threads
In a wool turtleneck under a tweed jacket. Such detail
Blurs in the profile between the lips as if parted to speak.
It seems abstract or like sunlight finally breaking through damp grass;
It could be maps cut up into little pieces rearranged
Not by cartographers but by poets and philosophers.
Larry kept pretty much the same layout for the other two
Conjurgraphs only he moved the dancers into Ngũgĩ's face:
Blotting it out with them. Then the sequence ends with the profile
Outlined but otherwise indistinctive in the vast landscape.

Sykes in *The World of Ngũgĩ wa Thiong'o* created
Images in themselves and not illustrations out of words.
Yet for the conference on Ngũgĩ' "Text and Contexts" the mere page
And its frame burst into three dimensions monumentalized,
Taking the form of two big and heavy works mostly of wood.
One of them looked back: a British classroom Larry imagined
Set in colonial Kenya; while the other embodied
Neocolonial meaning through a full look at the worst
African dictator garnished in his mock epic power.

In "The Colonial Classroom," Larry featured a window
Framing a bluish Mt. Kenya and the grazing silhouettes

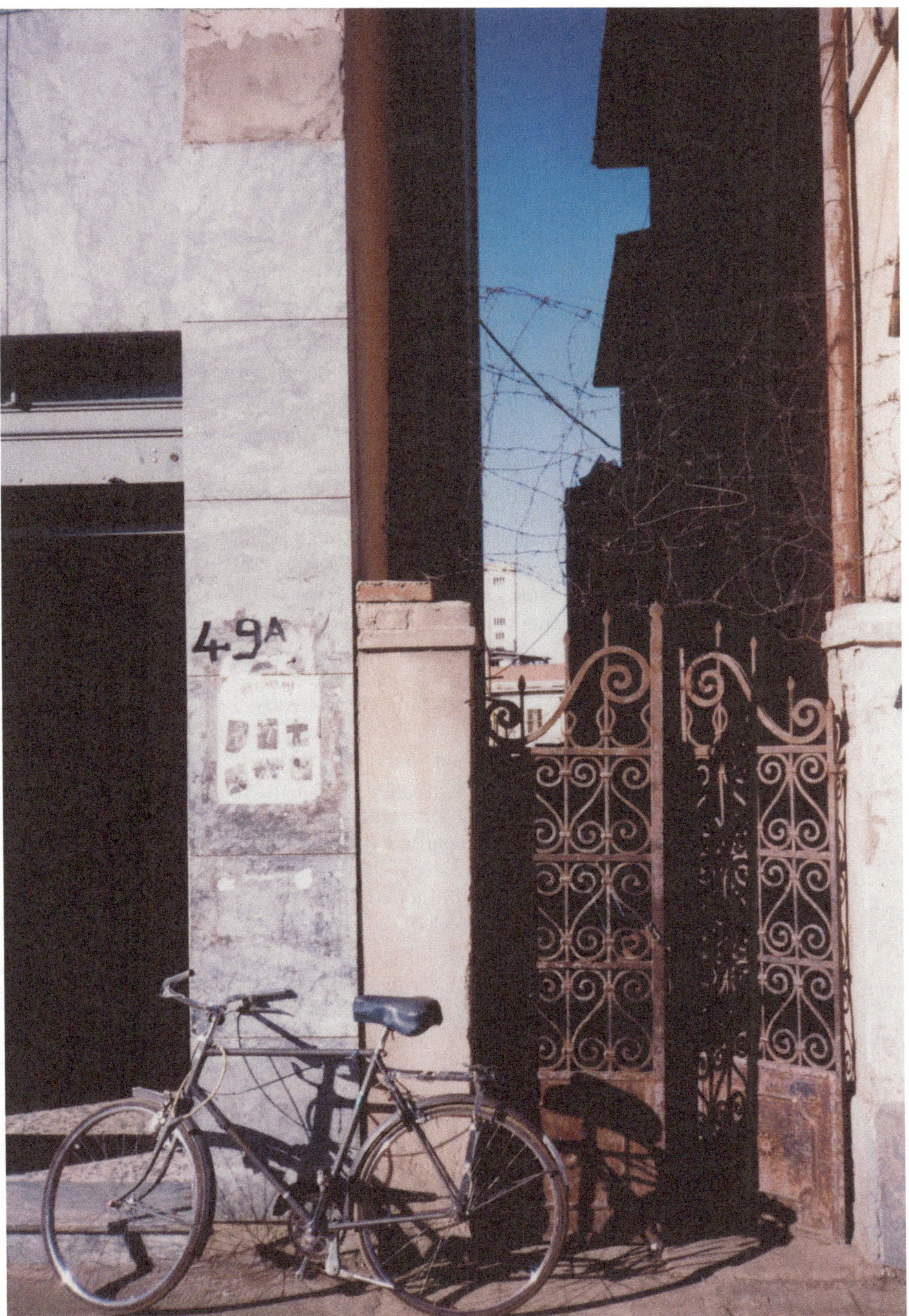

49A

Of several elephants set within green plains of a foreground
Scattered with bushes of fragile, lacy coral that could be
Out of the Indian Ocean. Nowhere else on the panel
Did Sykes allow much more consolation to the students and
Viewers invited to join the 7 x 5 slab of pine
For a few minutes of education, colonial style.
Flags of the nations of Europe who divided Africa
And a US flag to boot festooned the window looking out.
Two blackboards flanked either side of it, with "Good morning, Teacher,"
Written on top of one in a perfect cursive, while below
In the same handwriting was the conjugation of "to be."
England, France, Germany, Russia, Italy, United States,
Portugal, Spain, and more Western countries and their capitals
Took up the space on the other blackboard like they were enough.
Larry stuck teaching aids to the installation, including
Miniature microscope, sticks of colored chalk, field hockey stick,
And three transparencies, black and white 8 x 11s of
Great Britain's Parliament, Chartres Cathedral, and Roman Forum.
Meanwhile the window invited looking out on the landscape,
Hazy and lush blue and green instead of visual clichés
Merely to illustrate mundane walls of regimental rote:
Leaving no doubt about who's in charge and getting the message;
Not all that different from what Larry told me when I asked
"Now what does Scottsboro make you think?" the first time that we met;

Also not differing much – although the hand holding the whip
Was black instead of white – from what Ngũgĩ wrote about and Sykes
Clearly enjoyed in his life-size deconstruction of the tools
African dictators self-accessorized as homegrown rule,
When it was really a put-on, neocolonial gaze.
Sykes posed a full-frontal male in formal military dress
Taking up most of another massive, rough wooden panel;
Vertical not horizontal like his colonized classroom
And with a garishly painted background of green and orange.
Sykes took an upside-down horseshoe crab to make into a face,
Letting its pointy tail pierce a cockeyed, too small general's hat.
Emptily staring through eyes of cowry shells, the dictator
Sported brass merry-go-round rings hanging from both of his ears.
For a medallion he wore a nine-inch empty cartridge shell,
And for his shoulder boards, little scrubbing brushes did the trick.
Two oversized silver buttons etched with lions squeezed him tight
At his neck and at his navel in an officer's jacket
Red like the clay of the Serengeti when it's splashed with blood.
Two black machine guns – no more than water pistols – were his arms:

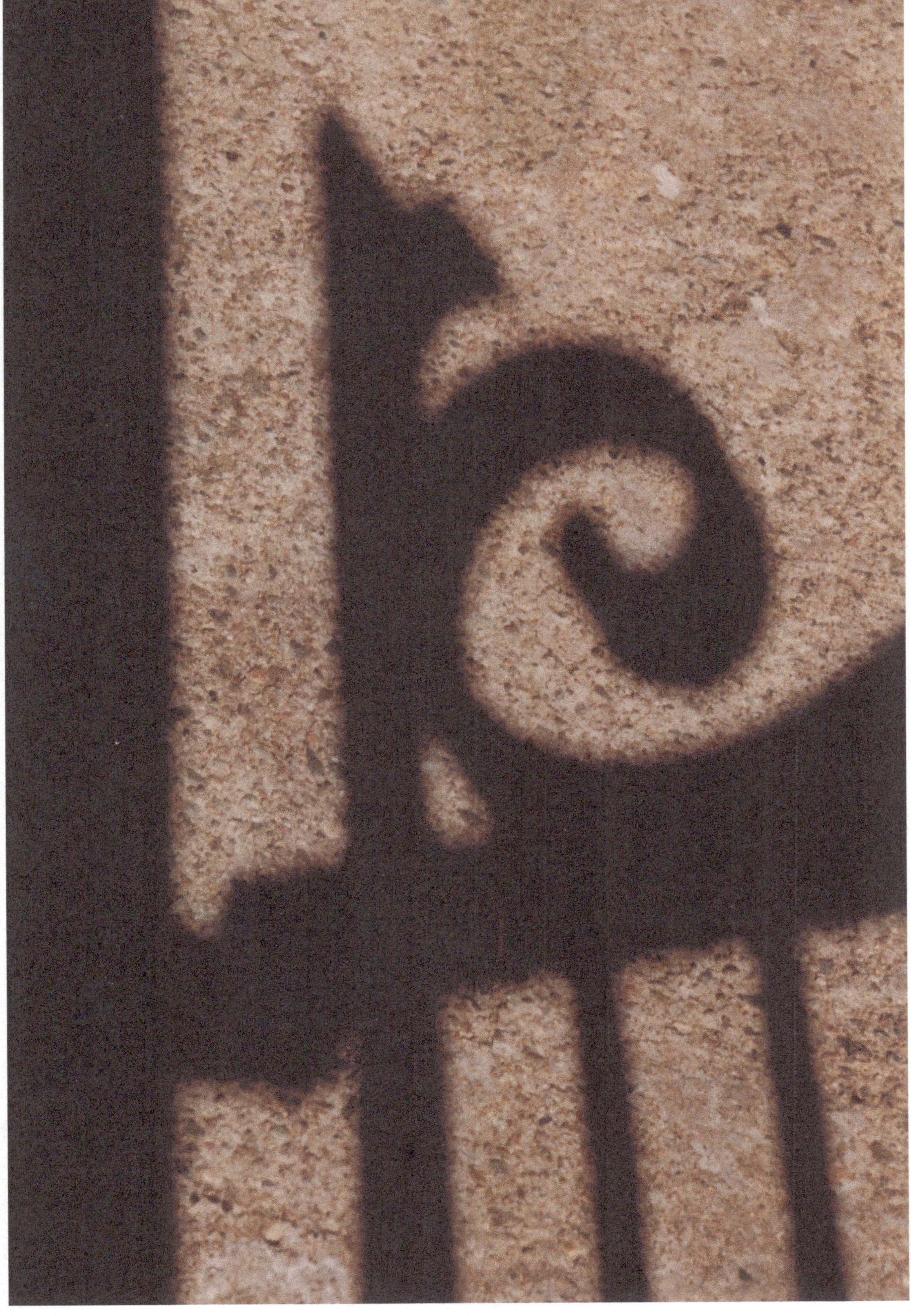

One pointing up and one pointing down as if in a shootout.
Hung from a much too cinched patent leather belt, his holster held
The very gun that I wore when playing cowboys as a child:
Silver and shiny, though also plastic; the legendary
Colt .45 – like the movies and the Wild West TV shows.
Not that this dictator felt secure enough with only that.
He had a couple of short and greasy, leather billy clubs
Stuck in the waist of his pants and reaching down his stiff thick thighs.
Nor would the dictator Larry saw as Ngũgĩ's nemesis
Manage a chance of surviving what Sykes also constructed,
Placed in an opposite corner of the one-room gallery:
Some kind of large box: it maybe held a refrigerator,
Prior to being transformed into a Sykes rocket launcher.
Heavily painted metallic silver, it had a gun scope
Made from a slide rule and aiming six fat, yard-long sharp pencils
Looking like rockets and ready for the dictator's next move.

Somewhere between the two, like that crow, *kagogo*, Larry tucked
Into his image of Ngũgĩ's profile through the prison bars,
Yet even more inexplicable, besides invisible,
Or like an egg in a body from the moment that's she's born,
Which could be fertilized, *Sykes in Eritrea* first flashed by.
It was the conference's packed and closing night reception, when
Ngũgĩ said earlier he'd invited Kassahun Checole,
Who was the Africa World and Red Sea Press's publisher.
And we should meet. When he introduced himself out of the crowd,
After I said, "Ngũgĩ told me you would be here," Kassahun
Answered, "I'm sorry, I'm late. He didn't give me the right time."
Hearing *The World of Ngũgĩ wa Thiong'o* was my work,
Kassahun offered to publish it and a conference book, too.
Both books were out a year later when I happened to tell him
I would be traveling to a conference held in Tel Aviv,
Called "Breaking Boundaries: Beyond the Land of Kush." Kassahun said,
"While you're in Israel, go a little further. Take some time.
Visit my country of Eritrea." That was '95.
Going then was like I found my picture on more contact sheets
Larry had sent me, but Sykes in Eritrea actually
Happened in '98 when we flew Lufthansa together.
Sykes took his pictures in Eritrea, starting another
Project like what I saw he did based on his meeting Ngũgĩ.
Only it grew into more. The Eritrea that Sykes saw –
Like no one else yet an Eritrea in its essences –
Ranged from the *objet trouvé* to conjured only as Sykes could.
Once more I witnessed a monumental Sykes portfolio.

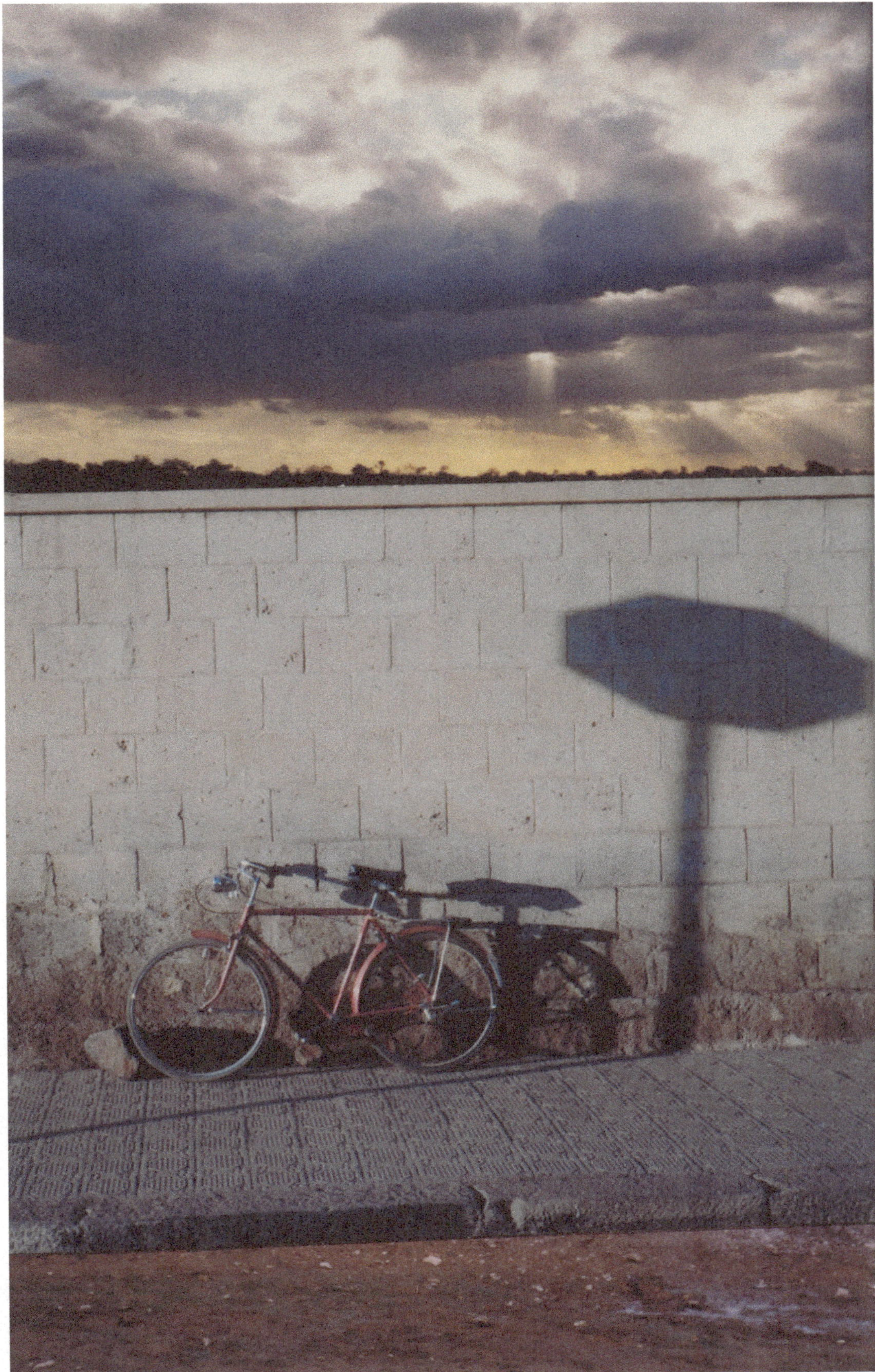

Some of it first appeared in Mkuki na Nyota's book,
Where War Was, published in 2016, a selection of
Poems I wrote about Eritrea and some translations
Of poems by Eritreans, modern and traditional.
Africa World Press would publish a new book of my poems
Several years later, and Kassahun asked me to find pictures
Which he thought would reinforce the poetry for a reader.
I thought of Larry: specifically, two images he made
Out of his pictures from Eritrea. Kassahun called me.
He loved an image of Eritrean men behind a gate.
It was a match for the poem, " Ngũgĩ in Eritrea."
This was October in 2020. Larry Sykes just died.
"He has a lot of amazing Eritrean images,"
I said to Kassahun." He replied, "We'll publish all of them."

Twenty-five years before, when I first flew to Eritrea,
I didn't know much about it, and I never expected
It would affect me so strongly, like the Ngũgĩ encounter:
How it grew out of an interview and academic book
Into a more comprehensive project, fueled by images
Sykes produced: contact sheets, inspiration, two people talking;
Two hundred more at the conference talking all about Ngũgĩ';
Visions and monuments based on his work conjured by Larry.
Still, the experience of first going to Eritrea
Not only led to a lot more – more than I ever could dream;
It led to more work with Sykes. There was no way that it could not.
Not only did he empower me in all the Ngũgĩ work;
I had it with me when I went to Asmara: the two books
Published by Africa World Press that I carried in my bags.
It had a bookstore and also published in Eritrea.
Yet Larry's contact sheets seemed to auger I could be there, too.
As they empowered my talk with Ngũgĩ leading to so much,
In Eritrea my entrée was my books under my arms –
Work that went back to those contact sheets that said I was allowed.
With that and with the books and desire for still more dialogue,
Yet with the contacts in Eritrea Kassahun Checole
Shared in a spirt as generous and trustful as Larry's,
After that first trip to Eritrea, I could never stop
Going back. Therefore, I had to make sure Sykes would get there, too.
Still, that was easy. Returning from my very first visit,
All of my raving, of course, made Larry also want to go.
It felt too much like a new home; he had to be part of it.

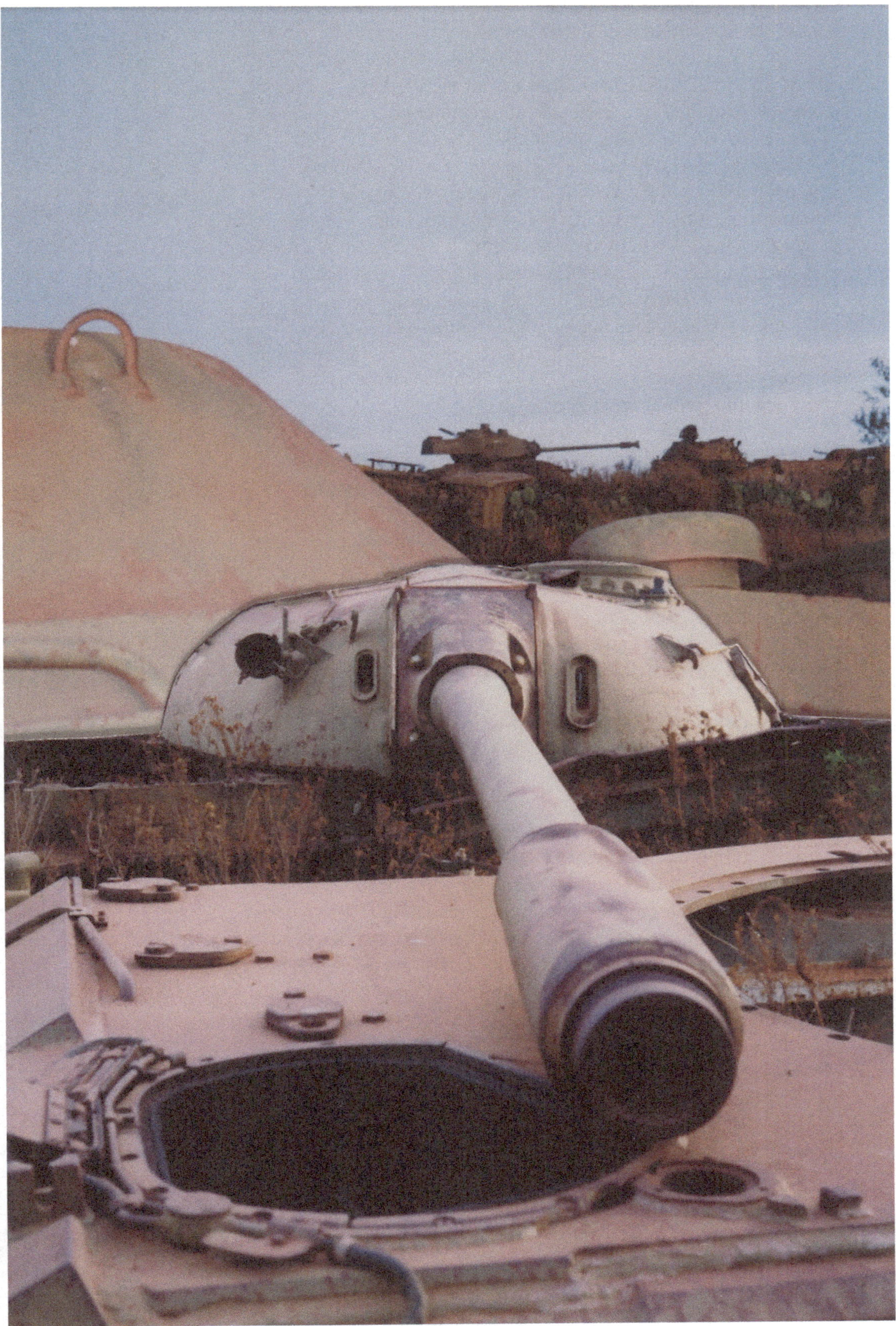

Traveling to Eritrea twice before I went with Sykes,
When I would tell him of beautiful or challenging moments
During the trip, he'd say, "Cantalupo, you like it too much."
One of his favorite phrases – "bridge too far" was another –
He even told me the origin that first time when we met.
I can still hear him, "You like it too much," saying it slowly
Over the phone when he'd call me from his basement studio,
As could I picture him smiling since he knew I understood.
In the mid-70s Larry taught in Kumasi, Ghana,
When the commodities market and inflation both were bad.
Meeting a well-off and old Ghanaian merchant while shopping
In Kejetia, the central market, Sykes light-heartedly
Scolded him over an item that he clearly overpriced.
Sheepish yet brash when he answered, "You're right. It's too much money.
I like the money. I like it too much," Sykes never forgot.
As we became friends, I'd even say it back to him a lot.

2002 was the most important "You like it too much"
He ever said to me. *Sykes in Eritrea* wouldn't be,
And my work in Eritrea would have stopped if he didn't.
Journalists and leading politicians in Eritrea
Had been arrested for advocating governmental change
In fall, 2001, after Eritrea went to war
With Ethiopia and in 9/11's wake as well.
I'd been invited around the same time back to Asmara,
Where I would edit and co-translate a new anthology
Of Eritrea's contemporary poets. Should I go?
I really wanted to. Should I under such circumstances?
Everyone with whom I'd worked since starting the Ngũgĩ project,
Also including him, answered, "No," and several of them said,
All my work over the last five years in Eritrea made
Me look as if I supported its political crackdown,
If I went back there again and acted like nothing happened.
I would become propaganda, as if there could be free speech.
This didn't happen and neither the anthology nor I
Served any purpose except for these great poets to be known
For the first time in translation and in their own languages
Not only in Eritrea but in the world of letters:
As in 2002 I expected, but how to be sure?

Time to call Sykes, as I always did whenever something new
Came to me. Since '93, this was a kind of ritual;
As would the idea lead to collaboration between us
Sooner or later (the poetry anthology did, too).

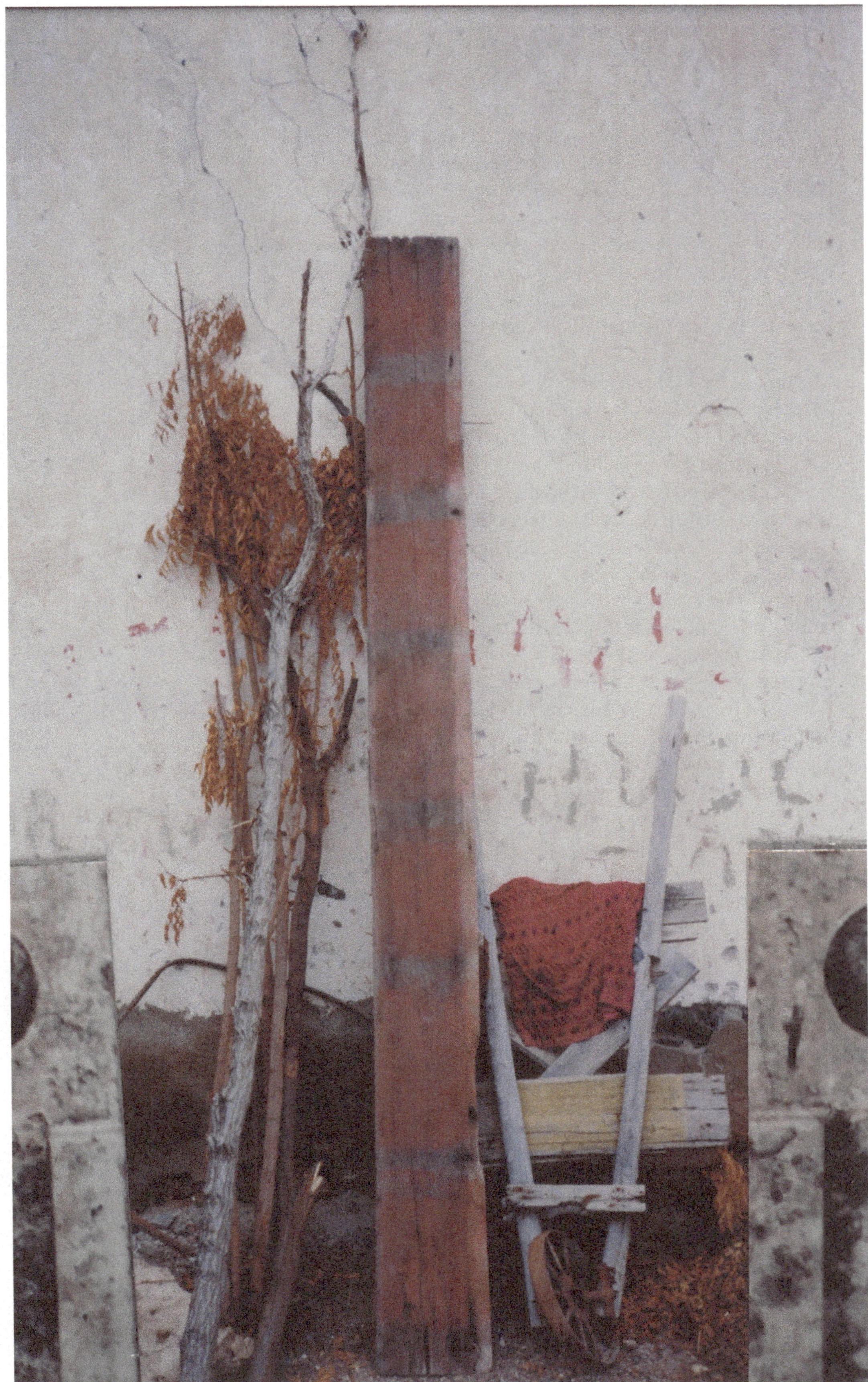

As I described the book and the situation leading to
Whether I should return to Asmara, no doubt Larry heard
More that I wanted to go than not because of politics.
After he chuckled, "You like it too much" several times, he said,
"It's a political mine field. If you think you can get through,
Why not try, when maybe no one else can. So, you must go back.
This is a part of the story you'll be missing all your life
If you don't." Nine years had passed since Sykes put me in the picture.
He wasn't going to tell me I should get out of it now.

Meeting in Frankfurt in January 1998 –
After he flew in from Boston and I had a flight from Newark –
Larry and I planned to fly together to Eritrea.
Affable with a distinguished bearing plus his being large
Frequently earned Sykes an upgrade from economy or coach.
When a Lufthansa attendant offered him a first-class seat,
Gracious and thankful, he charmed her into giving me one, too.
Not that he sought luxury. "He still lives in the depression,"
Barbara often said. So, the best hotel in Asmara
At that time, the Embasoira, built in the 1960s
Suited Sykes well with its tarnished mirrors, cracked leather sofas
Covered with sheets, the veneer all peeling, and the dingy light.
When we were back in Asmara two years later, I booked him
Into the new Intercontinental Asmara Palace:
Elegant, modern, pristine, and lavish; built by Italians,
And with no vacancies, it was so unique and attractive.
When I called him the next day, the desk clerk said he had checked out.
Nor did he know where he went. I called the Embasoira, but
He didn't go back there. Sykes had vanished into Asmara.
Next morning, I found a voice mail on my Intercon room phone:
"Come to the Khartoum Hotel at 1:00," which sounded like Larry.
In a back alley and small it made the Embasoira seem
Plush in comparison. I found Sykes there happily shooting
His Nikon 35 millimeter through old sheer curtains.

Writing about Eritrea almost nonstop since I went
There for the first time in '95, I saw three years later
Larry enthralled there in pictures unseen until they happened:
First in the light of Asmara, Eritrea's capital,
On a plateau in the highlands, over 1.5 miles high,
Filled with a mixture or *mista* of Italian Modernist
Buildings – apartments, hotels, shops, theaters, cafes, ministries,
Even a gas station – blending into local neighborhoods

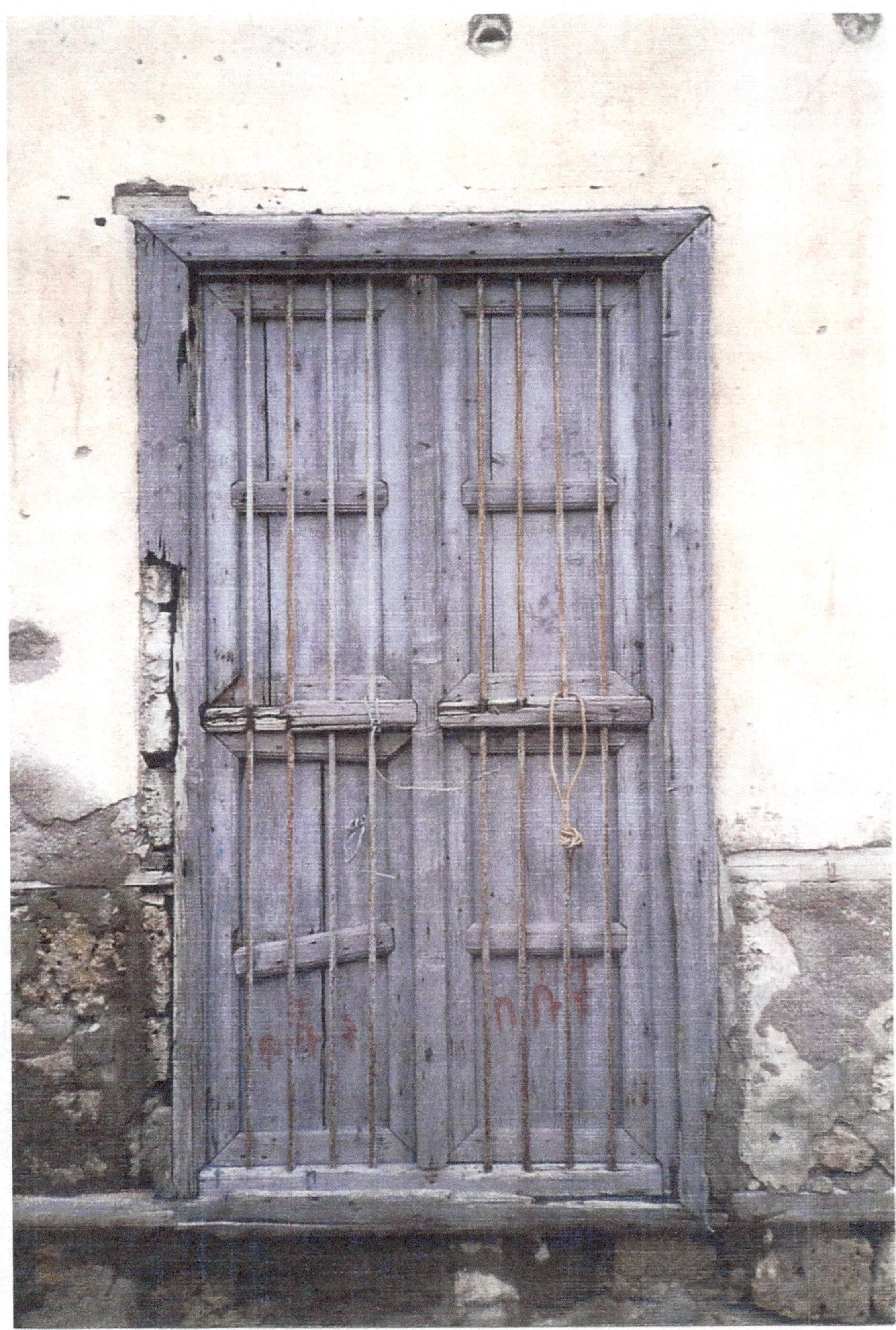

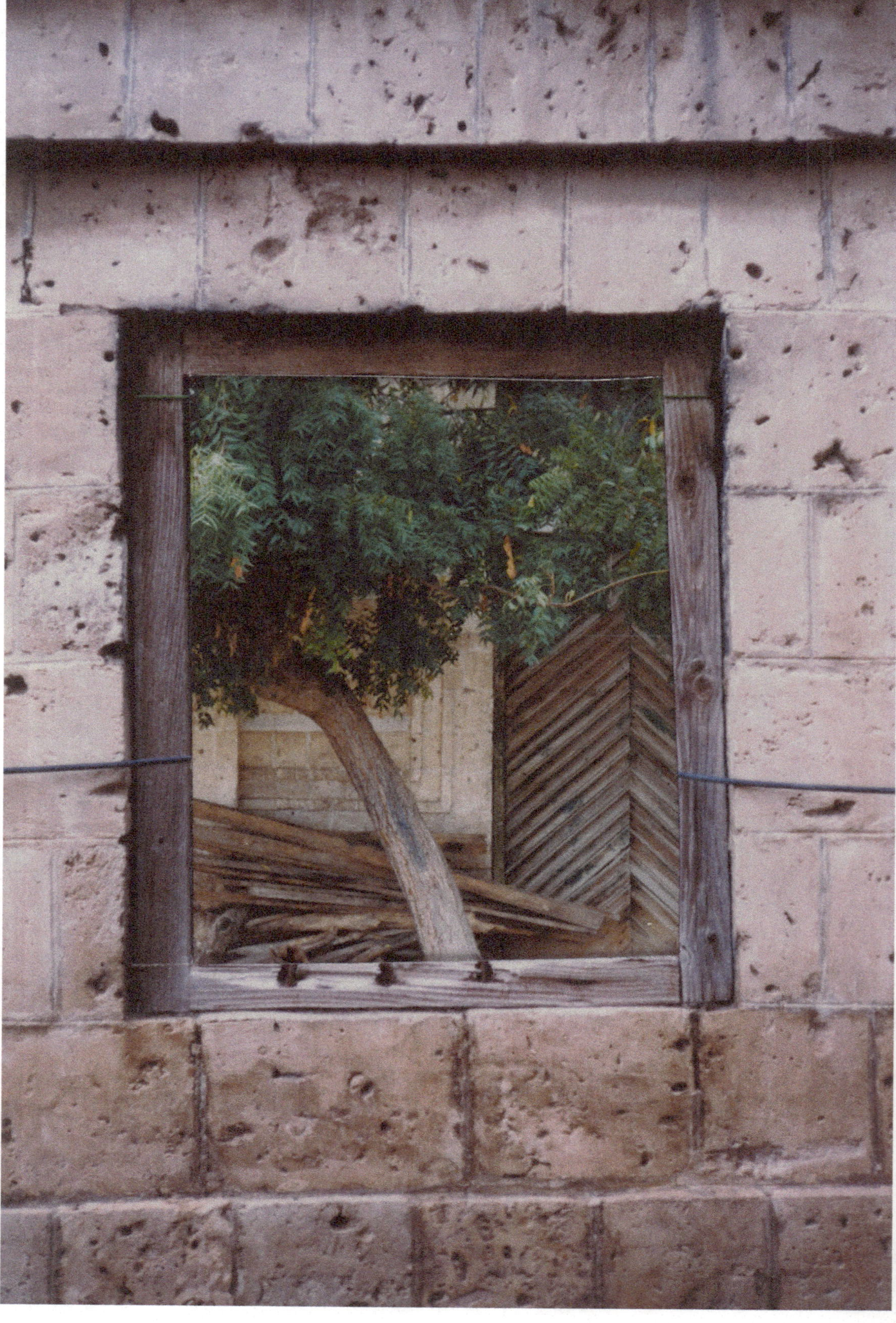

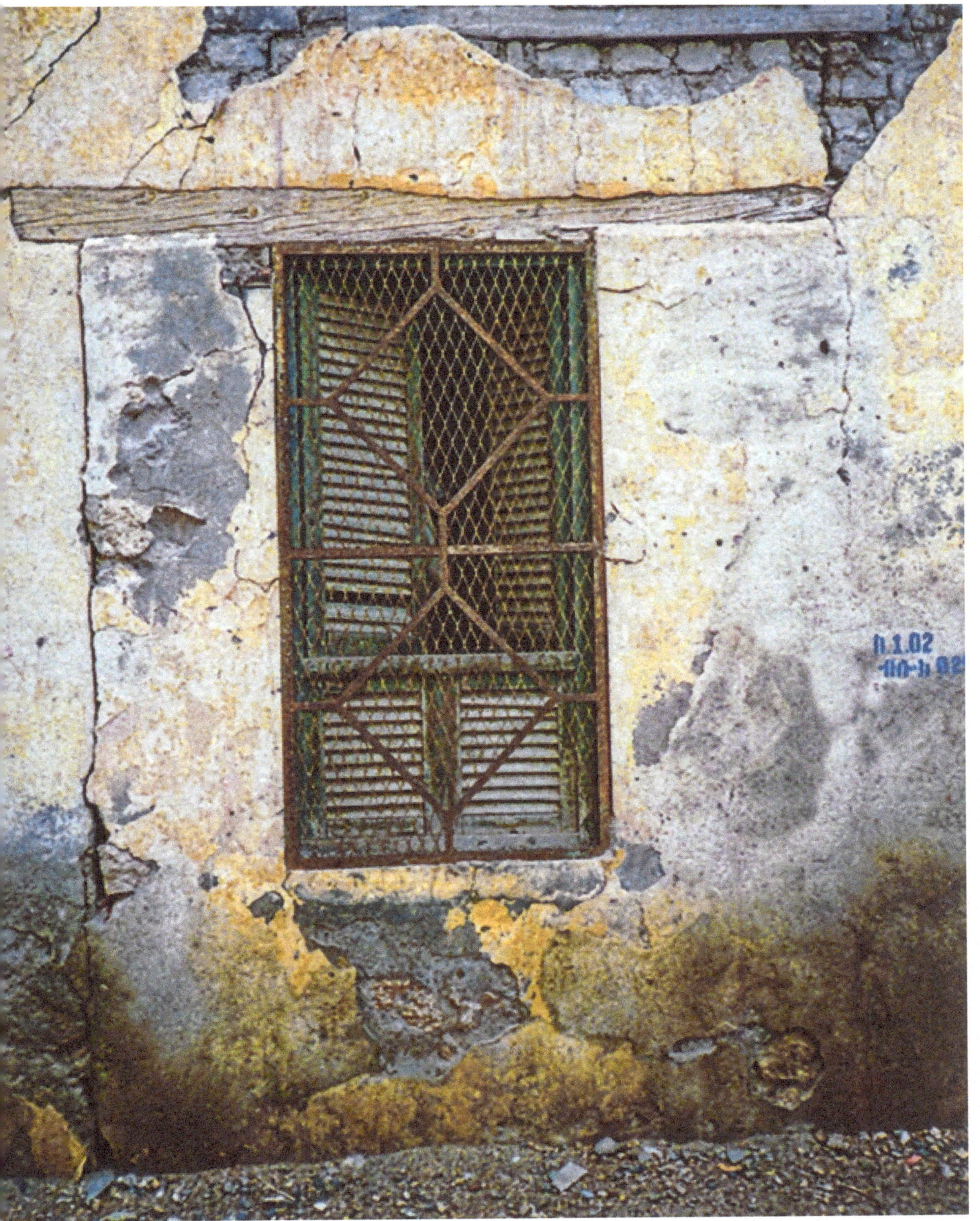
Ռ 1.02
-ՌՈ-Ռ 92

Varied and vibrant and safe as where we lived in the US.
Go to Asmara and it's all but inevitable that
You'll take a trip to Massawa, roughly seventy-five miles
Down an amazing escarpment to the coast of the Red Sea
And to Massawa, the port of Eritrea, colonized
By the Egyptians and Ottomans as well as Italians:
All of whom built their own versions standing next to each other's:
Most of them ruins of time or Eritrea's armed struggle
For independence from Ethiopia. Sykes went there, too.

Larry discovered his Eritrea in its passageways:
Doorways and windows and on the brink of outside and inside;
Taking the pictures unseen until they happened, even when
He alone saw them and showed us they were always happening.
Thus, people every day in a doorway could be there or not,
As could a tank from the war, a celebration, passersby,
Landscape or cityscape, empty courtyard – who knows when or why:
Really or conjured by Sykes yet absolute Eritrea;
For the occasion not existential or comprehensive.
If this were music, it would be chamber and not symphonic;
Or like a form of faith become knowledge purely visual,
Whether it's substance or not or evidence of anything
Other than some kind of story untold still to be assured
Endlessly through its allure Sykes focused in Eritrea.

Not without knowing the shootings, clubbings, mass graves, detentions,
Genocide, pogroms, beheadings, bombings, torture, kidnappings,
Fevers, starvation, and war within these very same pictures.
All of it happened, they said. It wasn't under the surface.
That's what the surface was made from here. What else would it look like?

Sykes and I walking together traded images and words
Trying to join them together so that we could maybe see
How an epiphany happens, or so he saw Massawa:
Doorway to doorway of layer after layer hard to tell
If they'd become total ruins or if they'd been born again;
Whether Egyptian, Italian, British, Turkish, Amharic.
Marble or coral walls made no difference to the cluster bombs
Pockmarking everywhere if it wasn't rubble already.
Where a mosque crumbled a palm tree had become the minaret.
One of the doorways that could have been ecclesiastical
Looked like it could be a gate to heaven made of splintering
Weathered planks, plywood, and rusty sheets of metal falling short

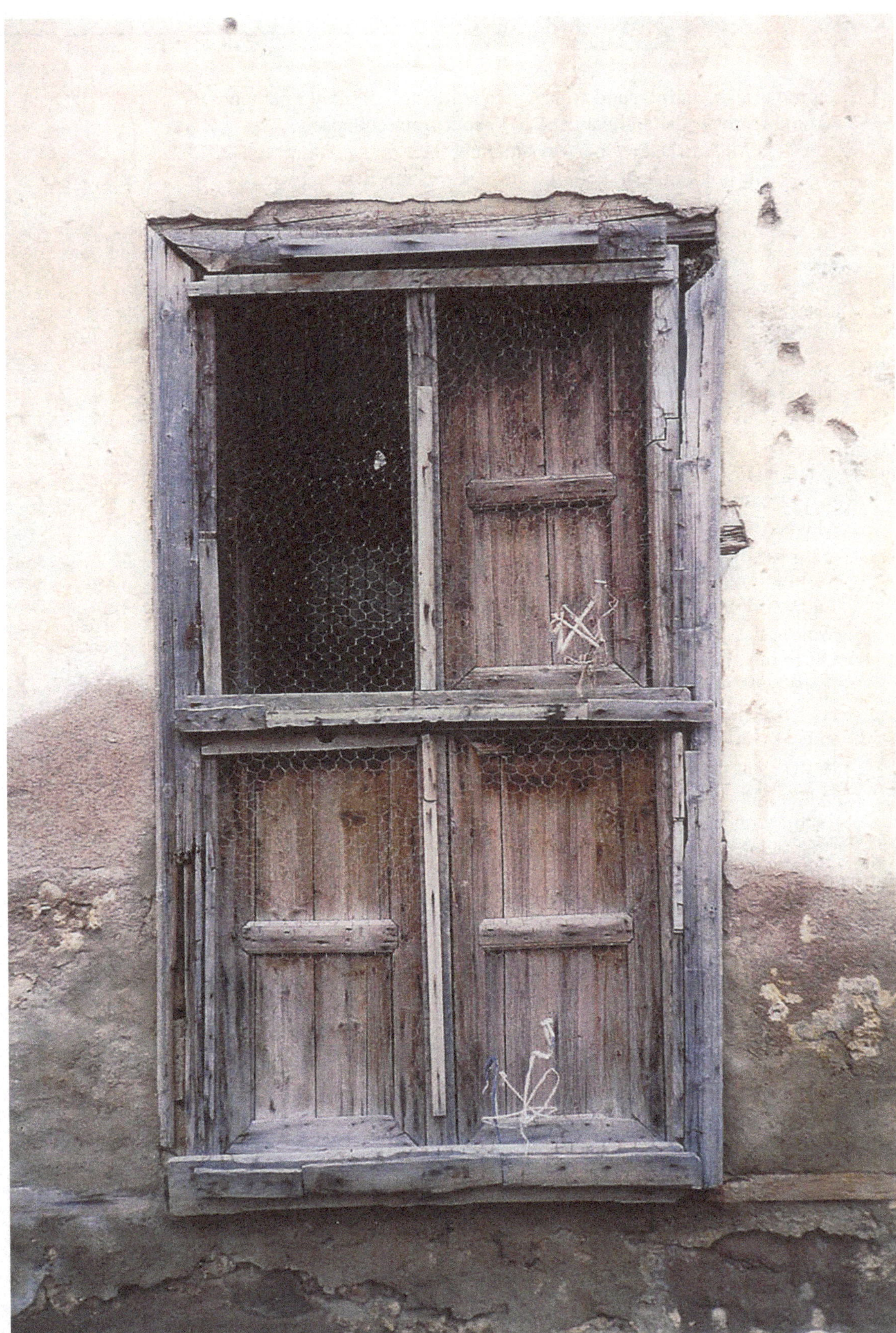

Of the bricks, marble, and stucco patched with yesterday's cement
Trying to cover the archway and to keep it from collapse.
Sykes in Massawa saw doorways making their own conjurgraphs.
Heaven or holding back hell; the Horn seems rarely in between
Yet without certainty which side of the door contains hell more.
So said another door arching high but nearly blocked with rocks.
Forty sheets of corrugated metal and several tree trunks
Made sure it stayed shut, while down the street what looked like a gateway
Perfectly balanced its lintel set in stuccoed over blocks
Carved out of coral where five big planks of wood a rusty blue
Shut every possible angle in or out but just in case,
They had been hammered with nails at random aimed at some stray chance.

Window to window, too, in Massawa Sykes found the unseen
Conjured when he snapped his Nikon 35 millimeter.
Maybe there had been some glass but not a shard or glint remained,
As if the dictum that "for now we see through a glass darkly"
Wouldn't apply to these frames and what was really there or not.
Larry shot trees through them, tanks about to fire, children playing.
Wood piles, a veiled woman walking by herself behind the tank;
Off in the distance a column from an ancient Red Sea site.
None of it quite made sense. Not a single frame looked like inside.
As I've said, Sykes found his Eritrea mostly on the brink,
In between outside and in, and when I joined him there, I saw
Better than ever why he said in our very first meeting,"
"I take the picture I don't see till it happens." Sykes would find
Conjurgraphs waiting to happen even in the window frames
Boarded up tightly and further blocked with iron bars and wire.
Twisted twine, bundles of little sticks, dry flowers, a feather,
Bunches of red and black berries, shreds of brightly colored silk,
Leaves in a half-ripped bag, and a strand of useless tiny stones:
How did they happen to be there as if conjured out of air
At the same moment that Larry recognized they should be there
And took the picture: like when he saw the archways still rising
Inside an otherwise big and bombed-out Massawa building.
While Sykes took pictures the space would not be what they were about.
At the same time a boy ran in looking for his soccer ball:
Not seeing Sykes and Sykes neither seeing him until he was
There in the shot. Larry caught him with his ball in the rubble
And when he ran out, a lot like Larry did in Scottsboro
And then in Baltimore: boy and ball and taking on the world.

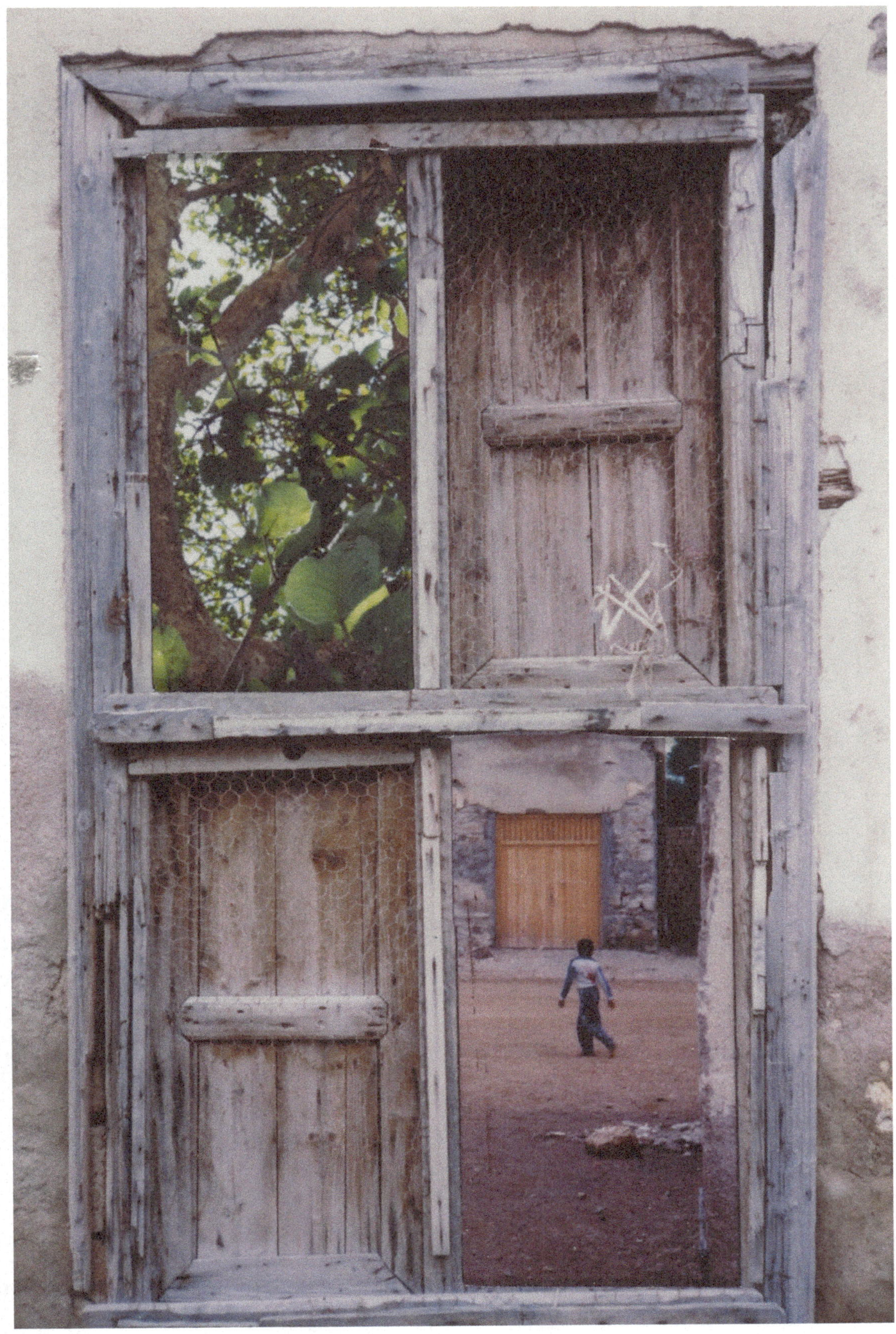

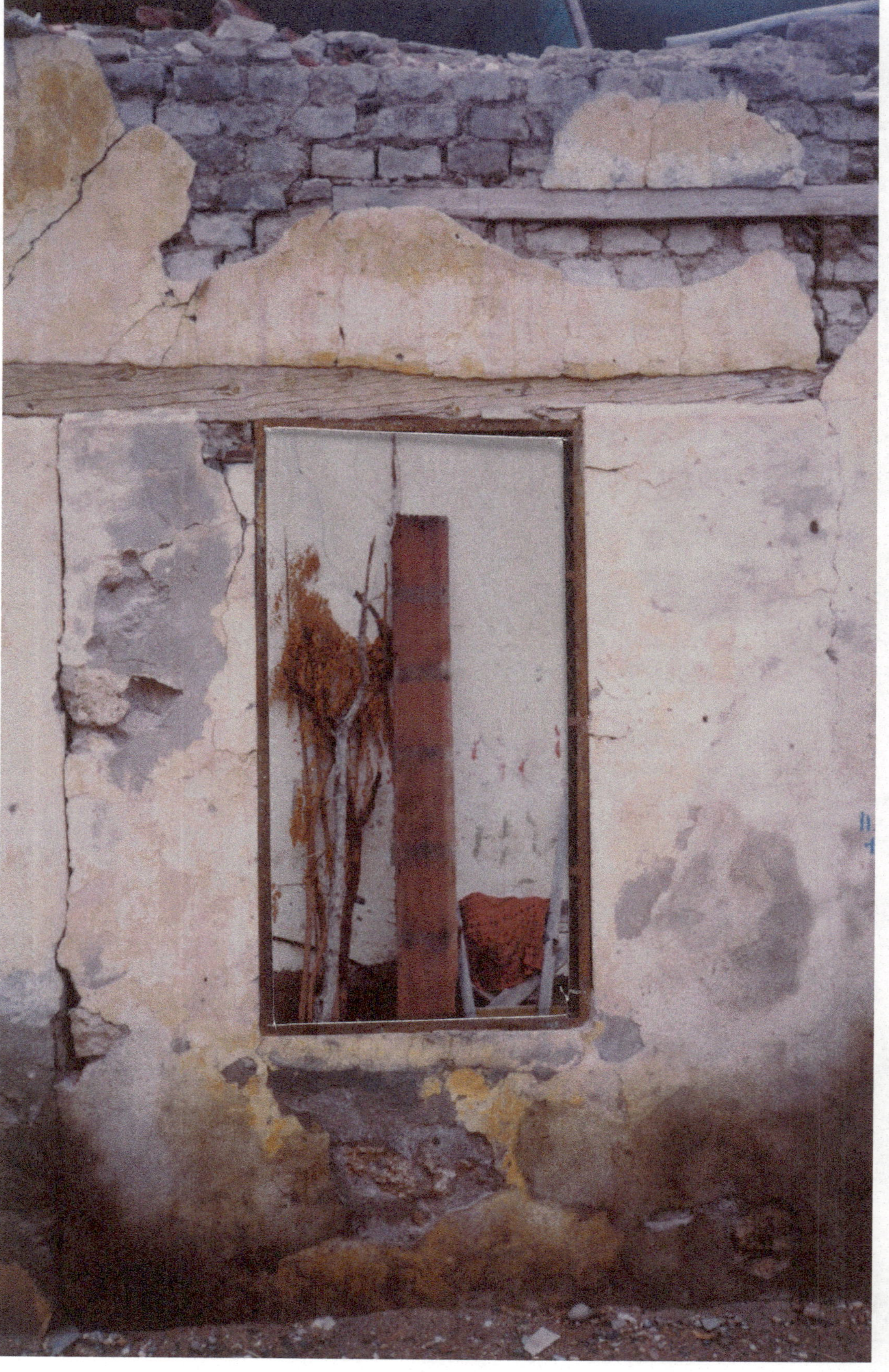

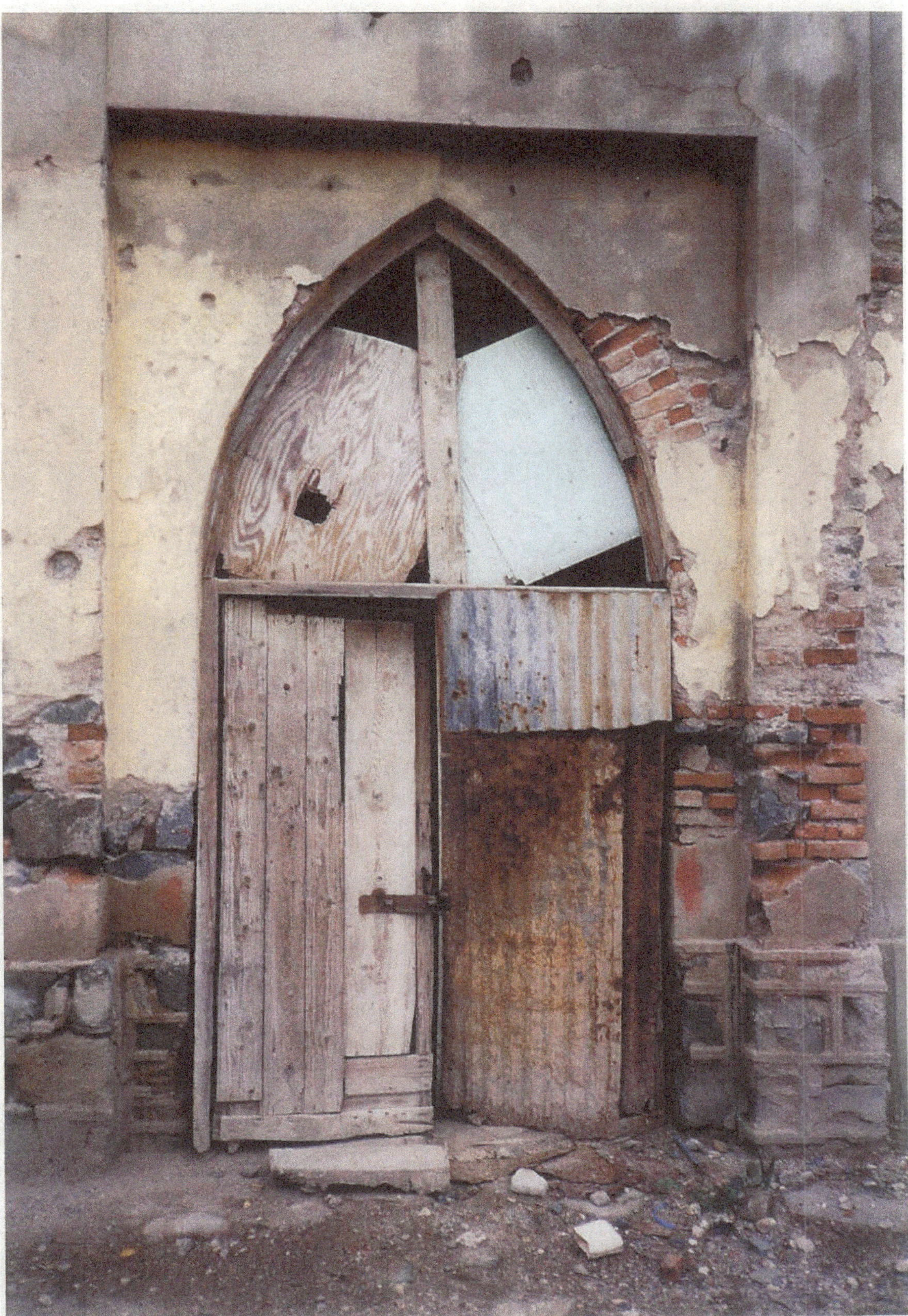

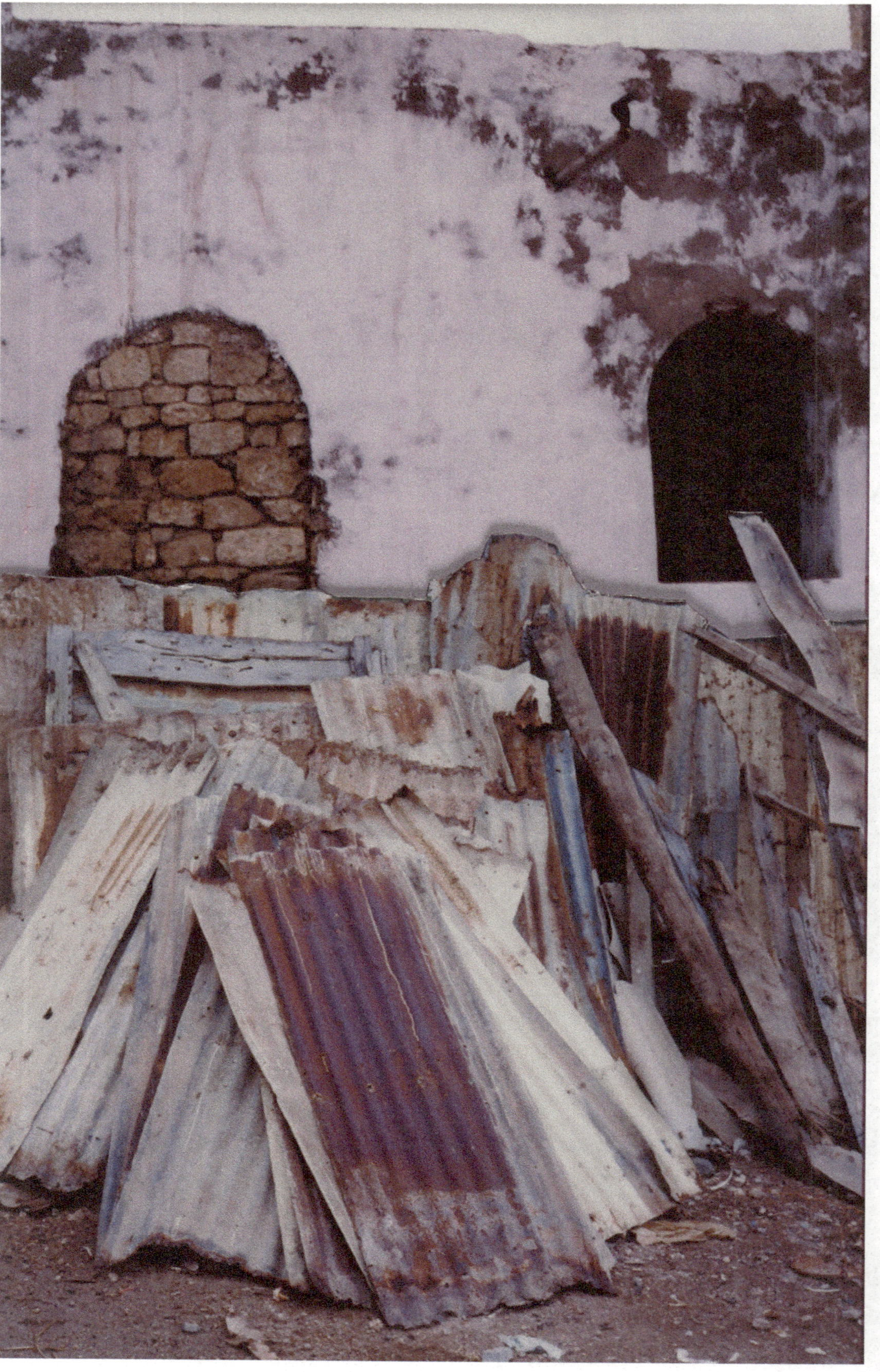

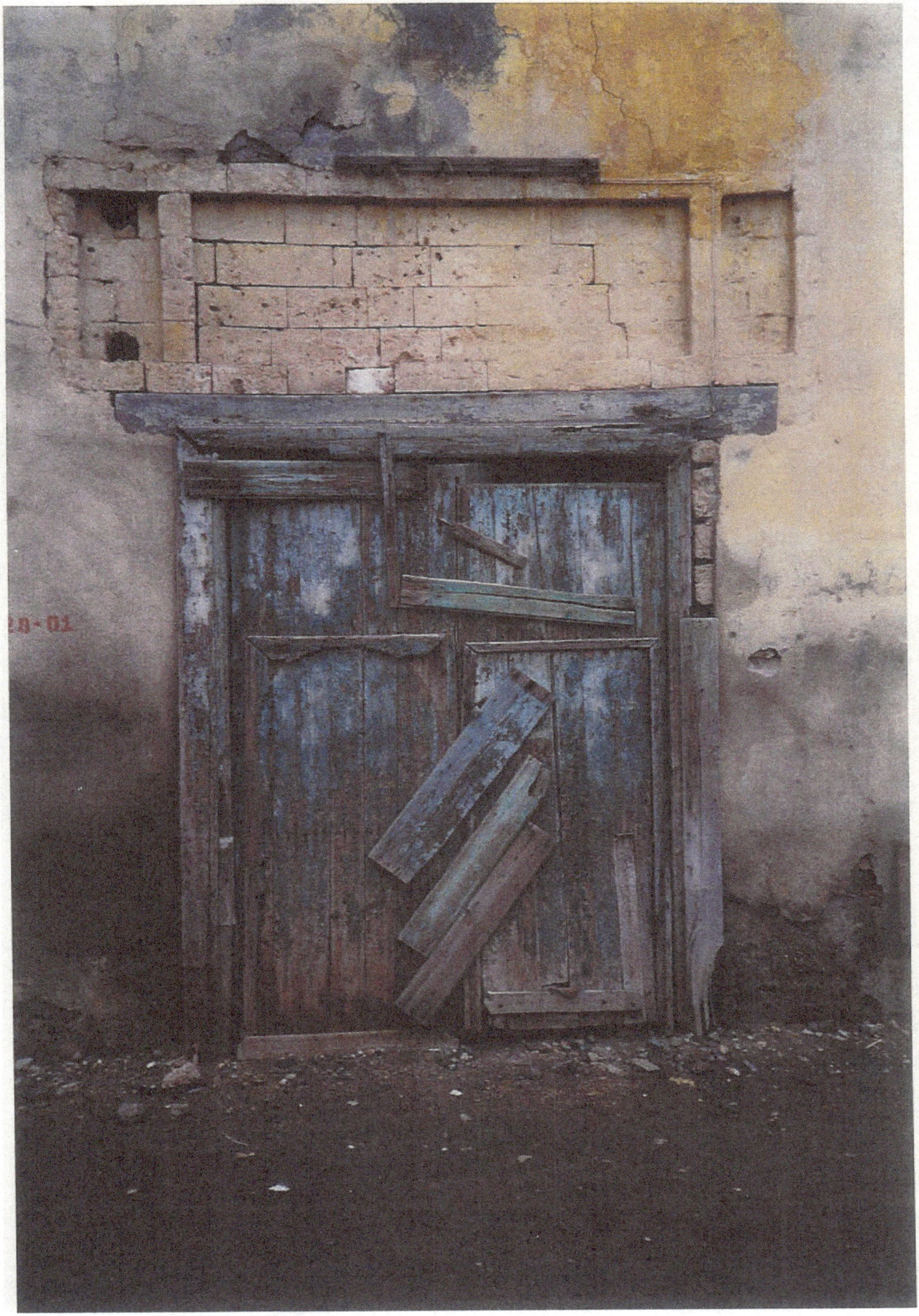

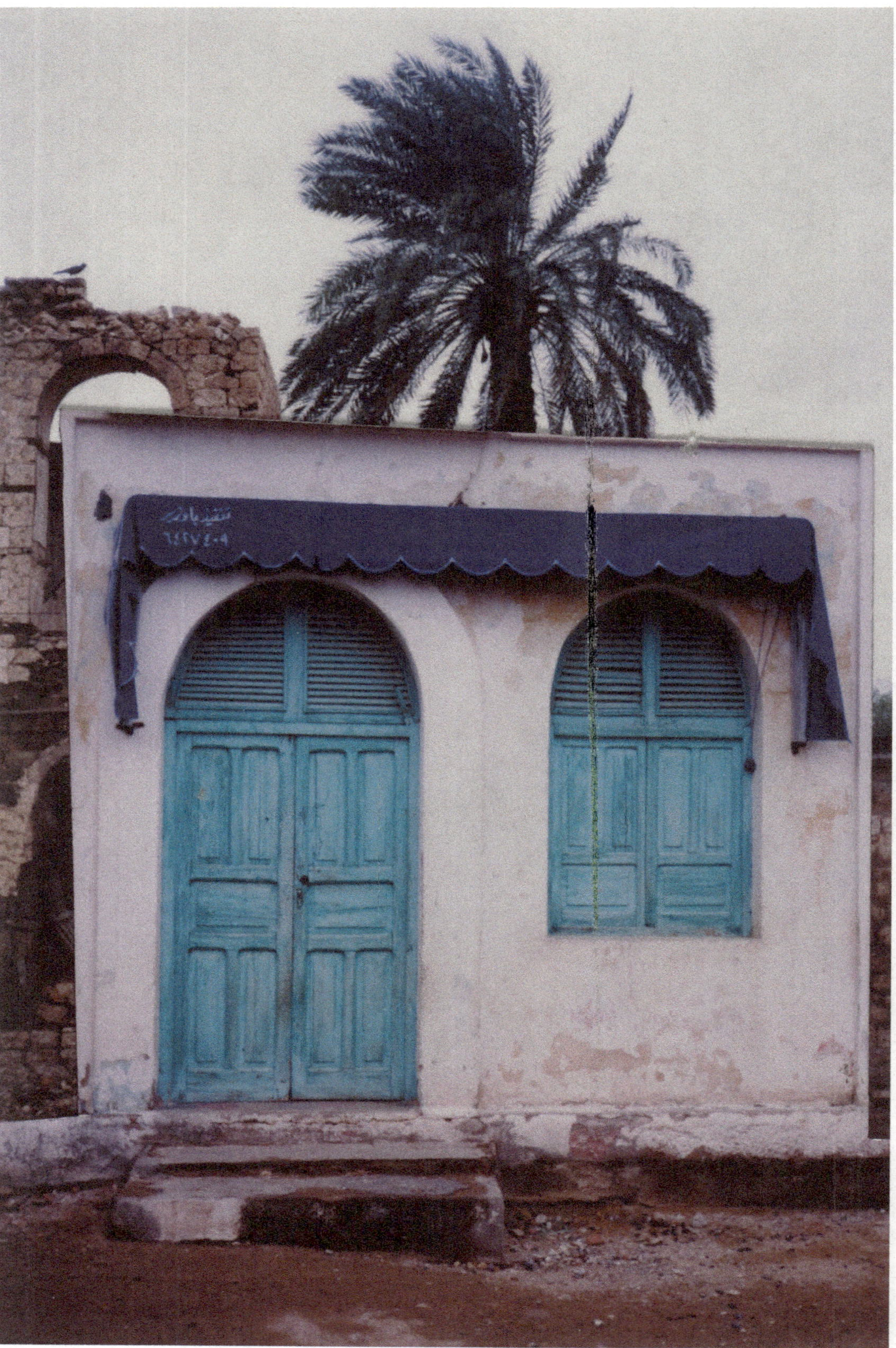

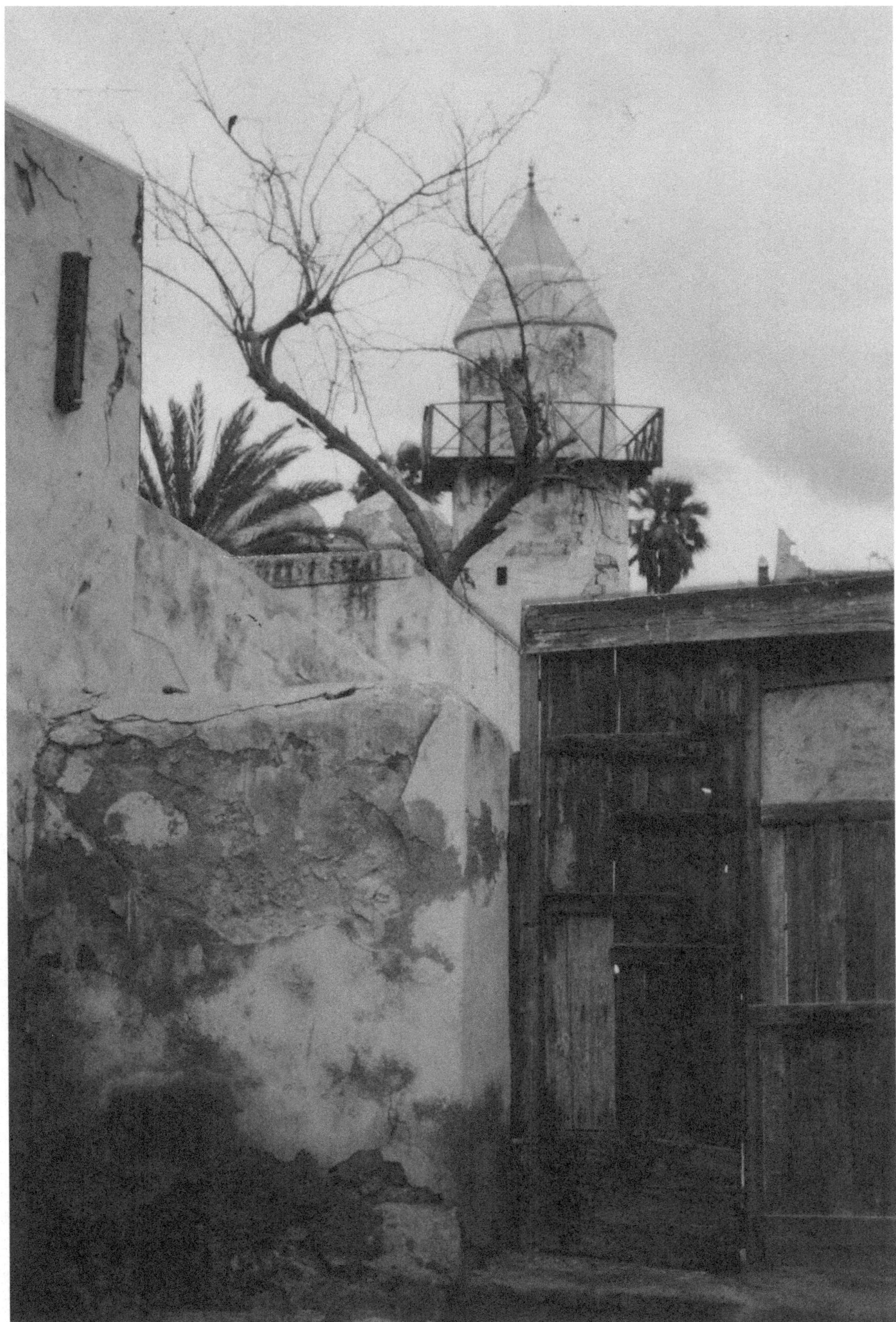

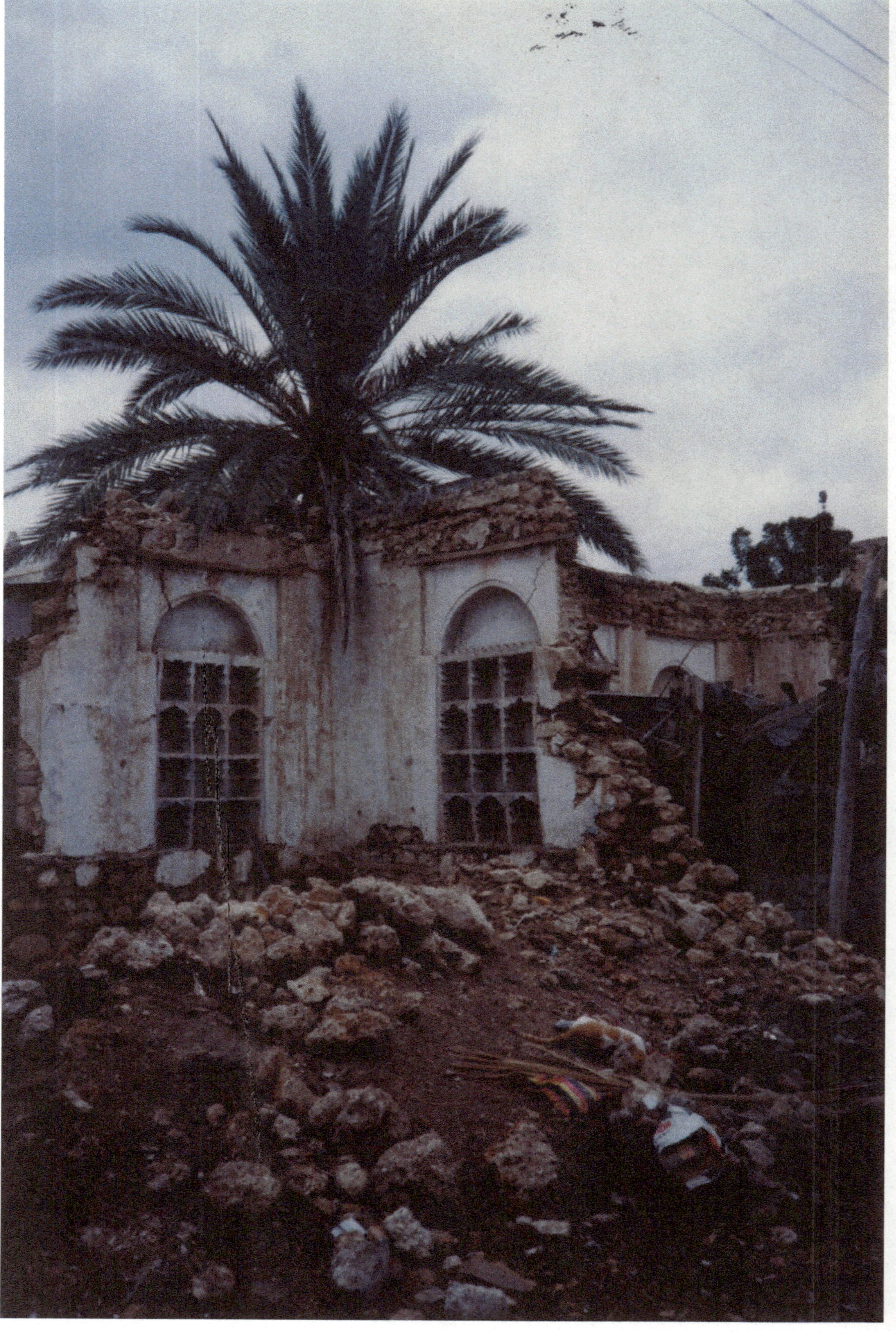

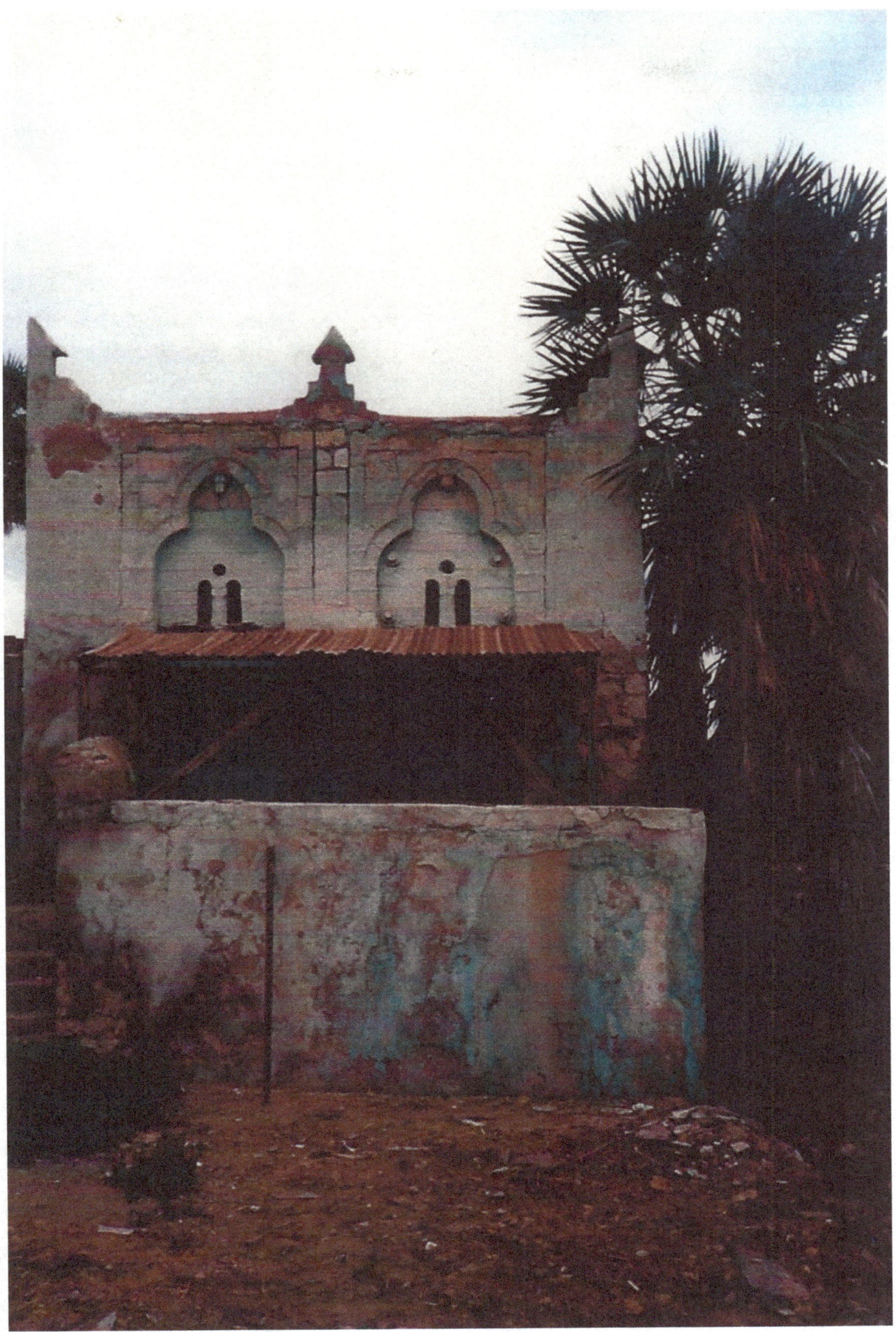

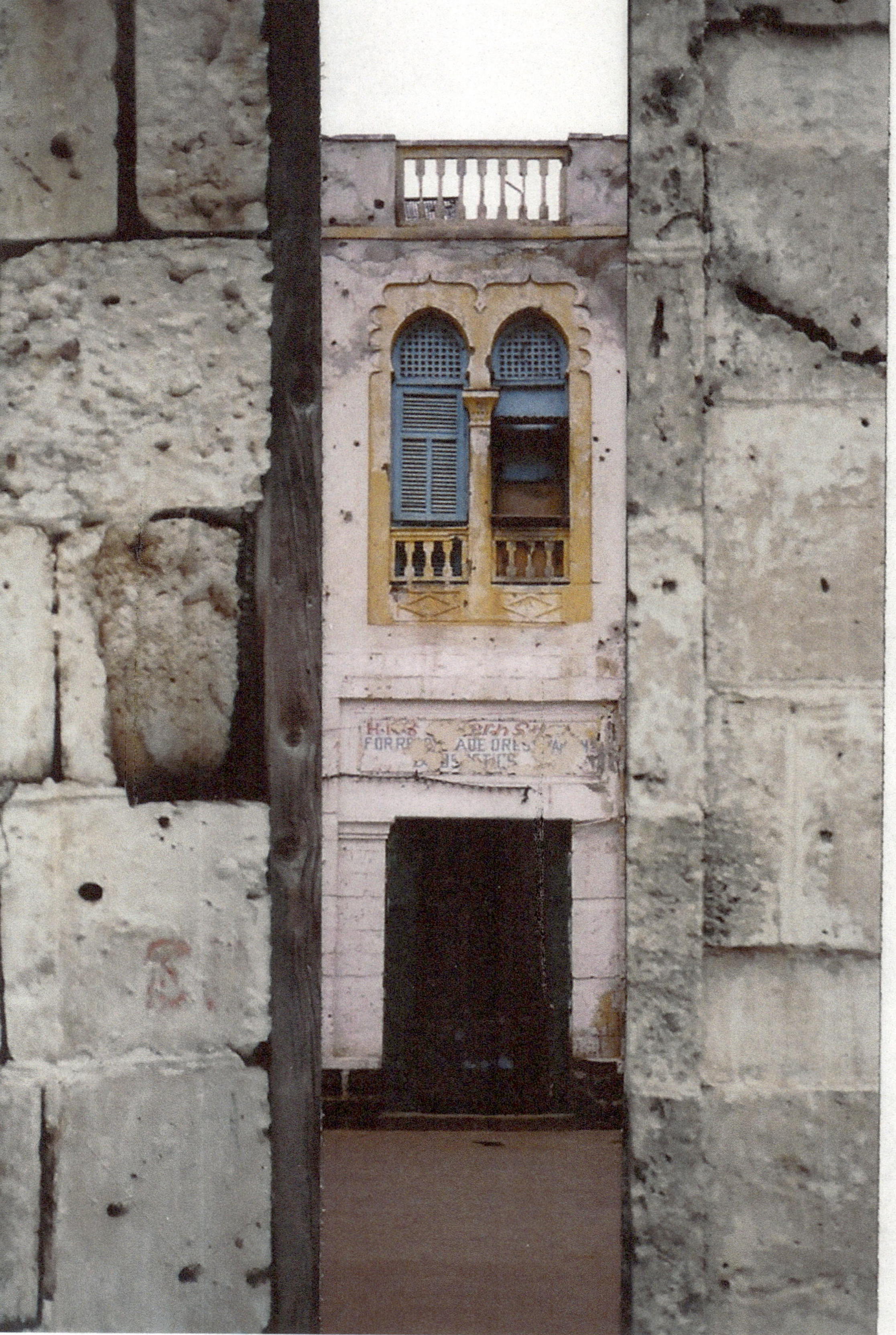

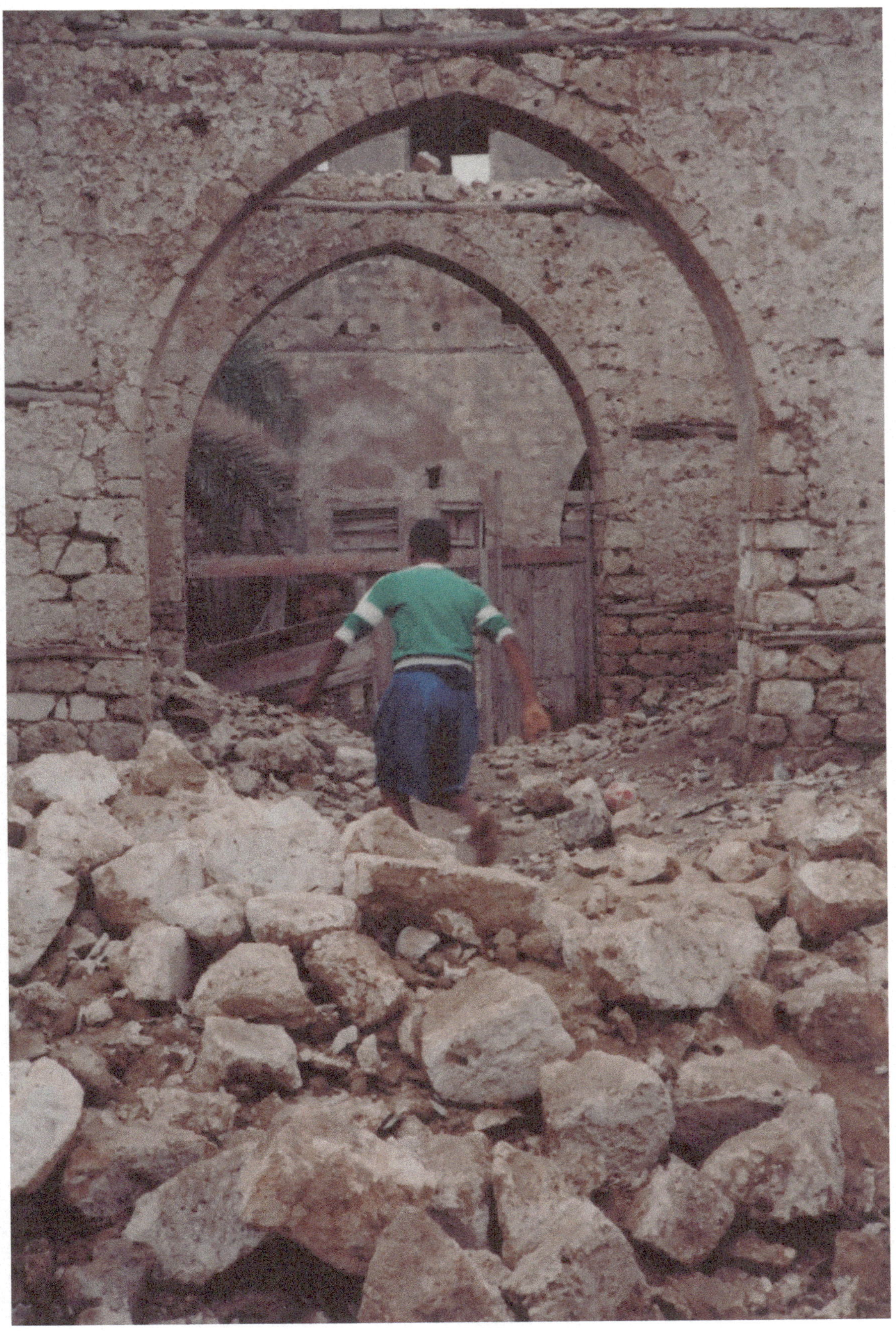

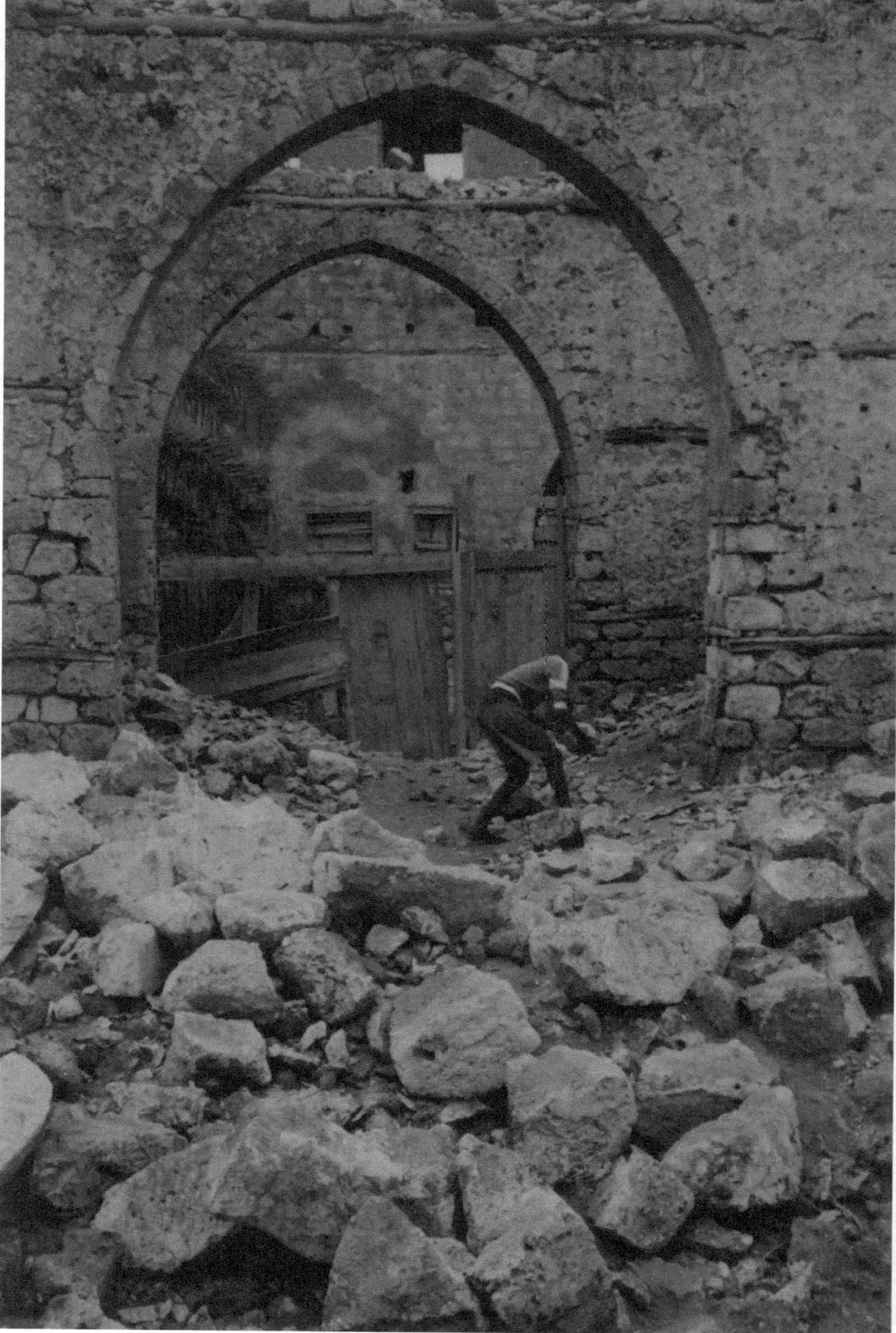

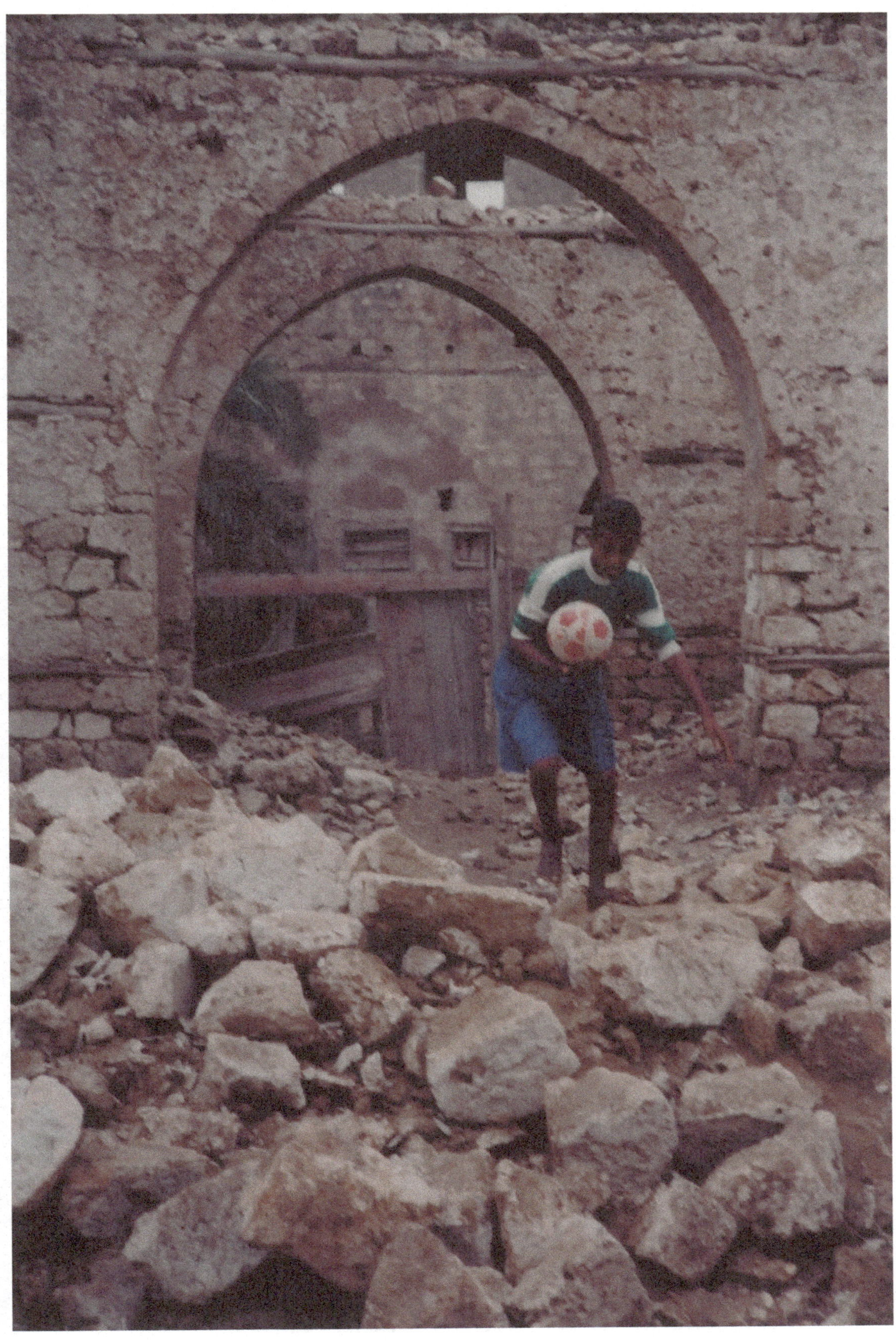

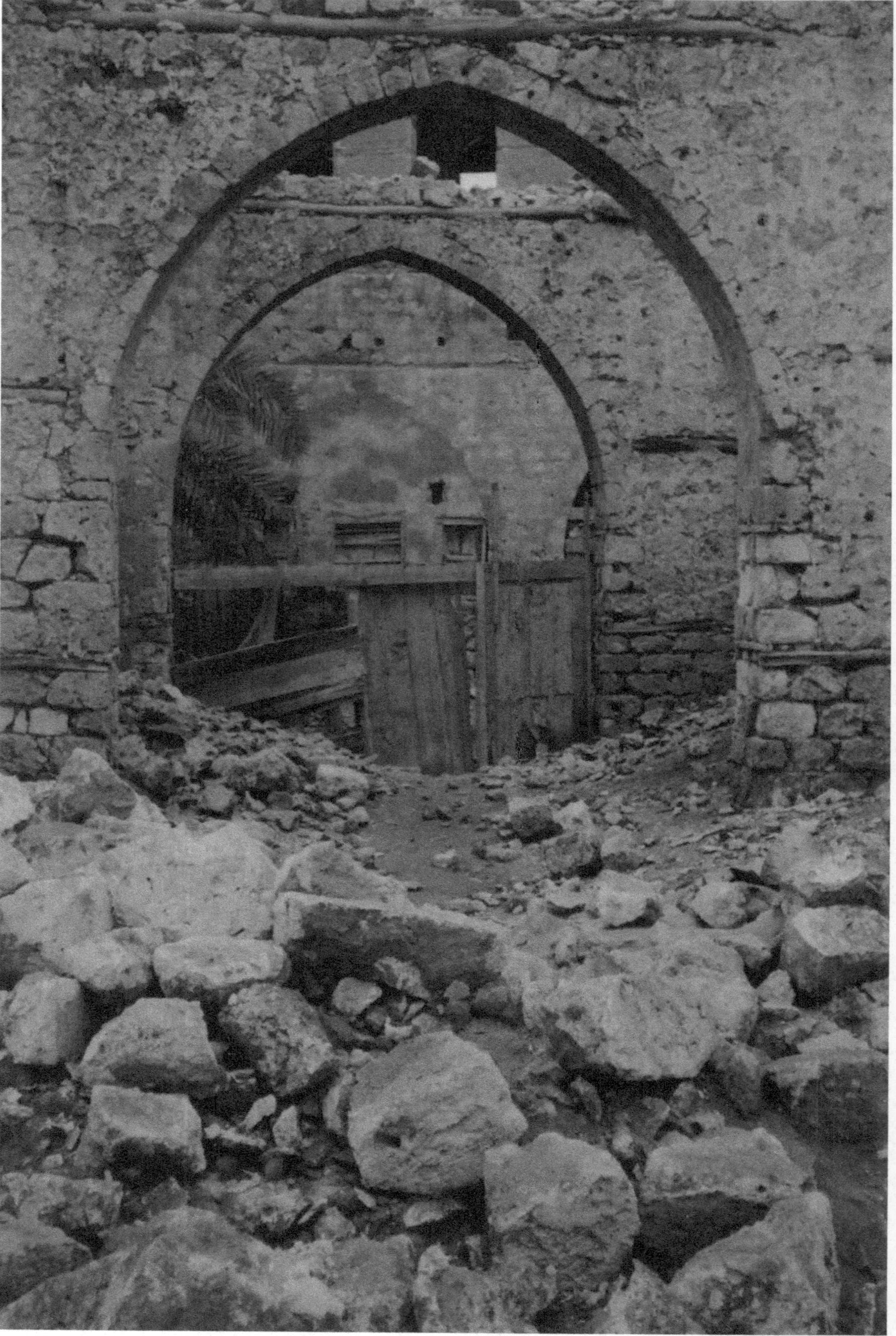

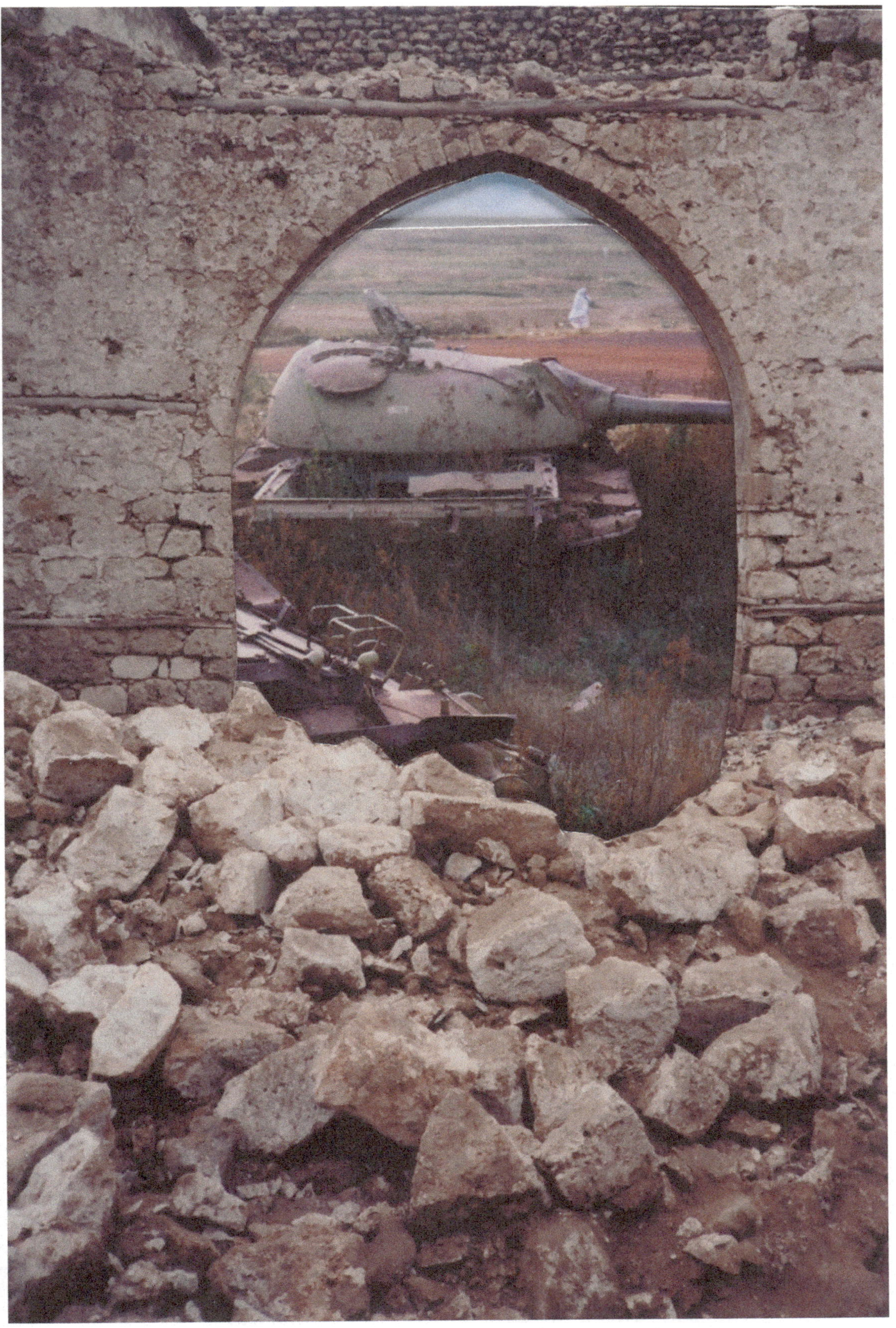

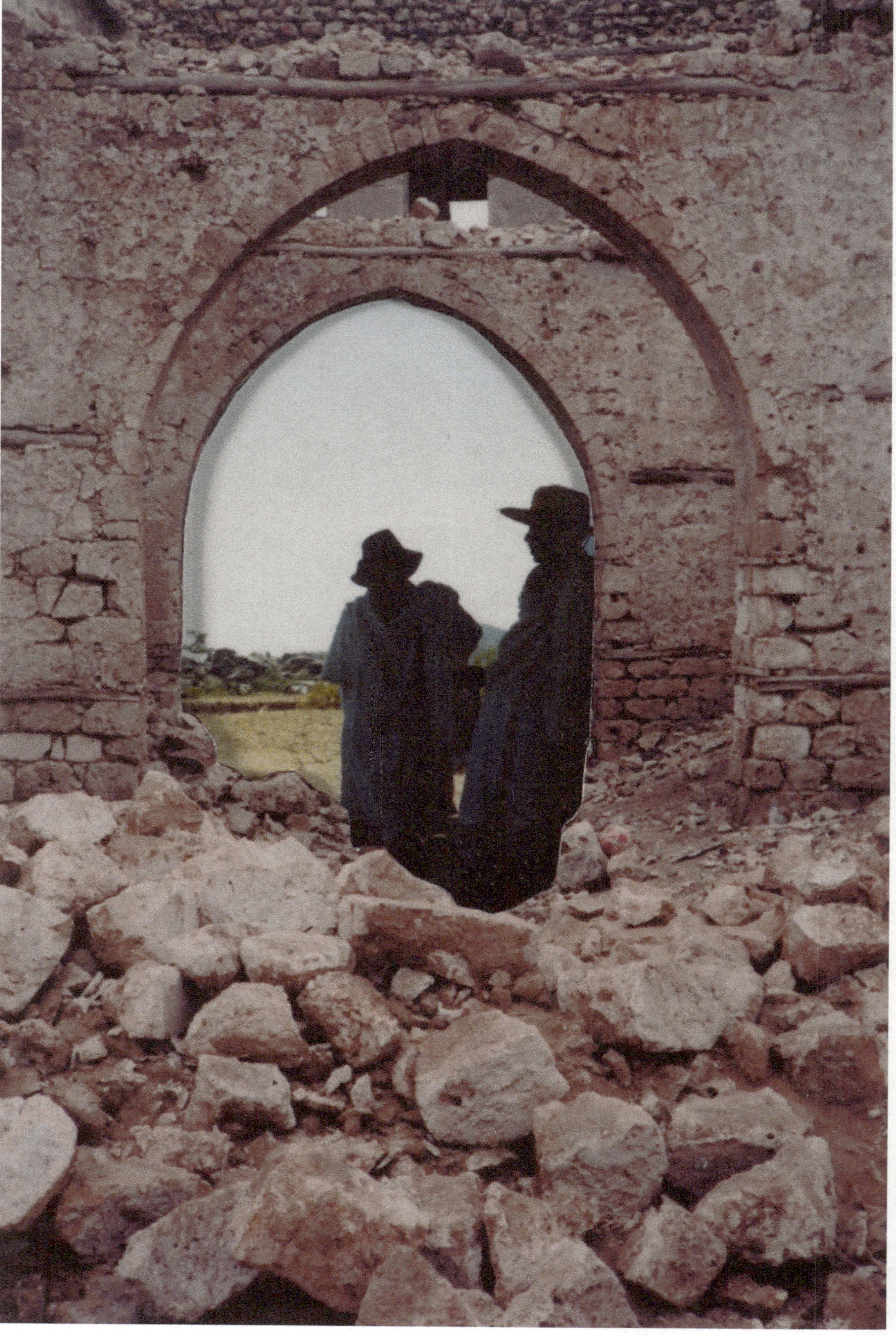

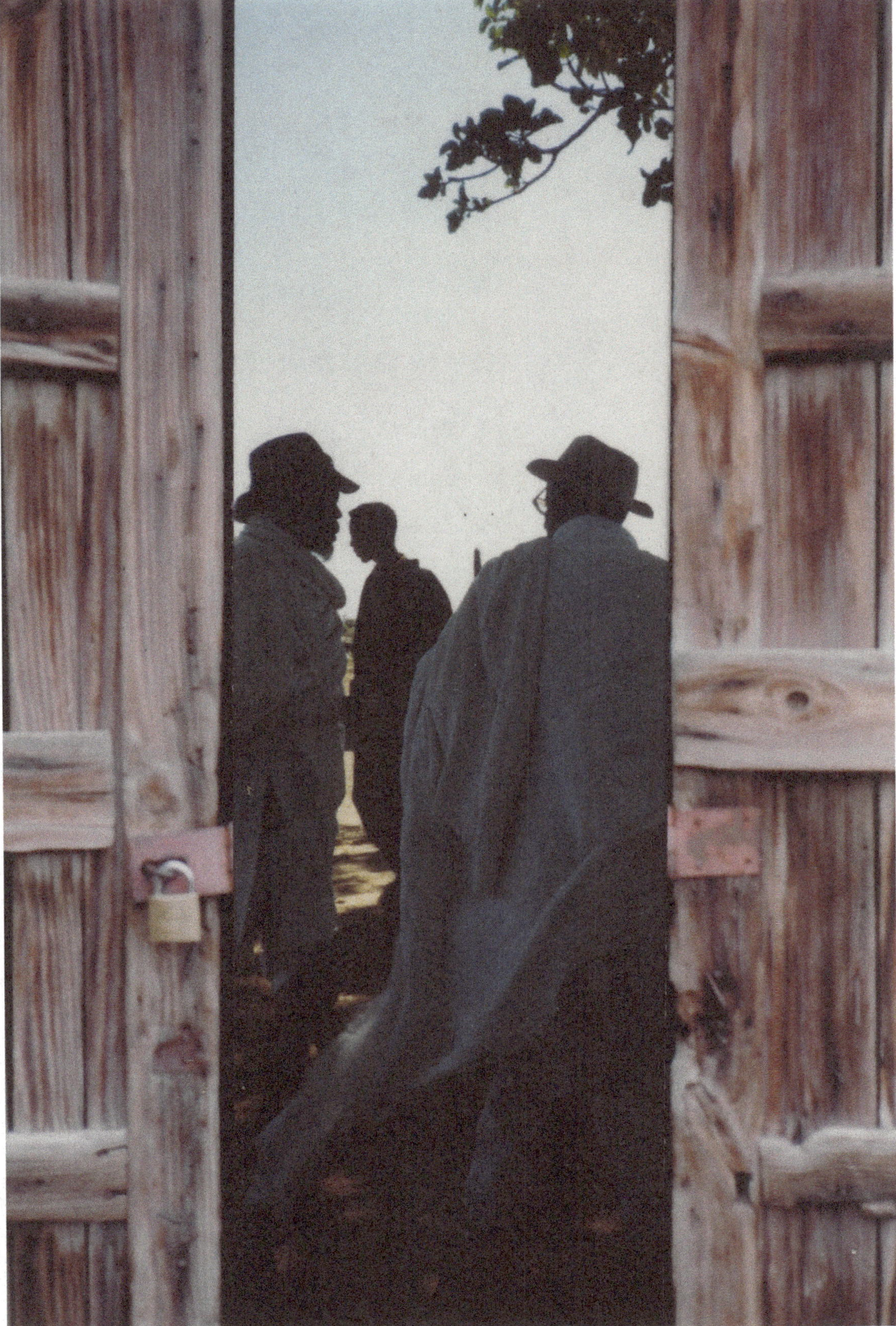

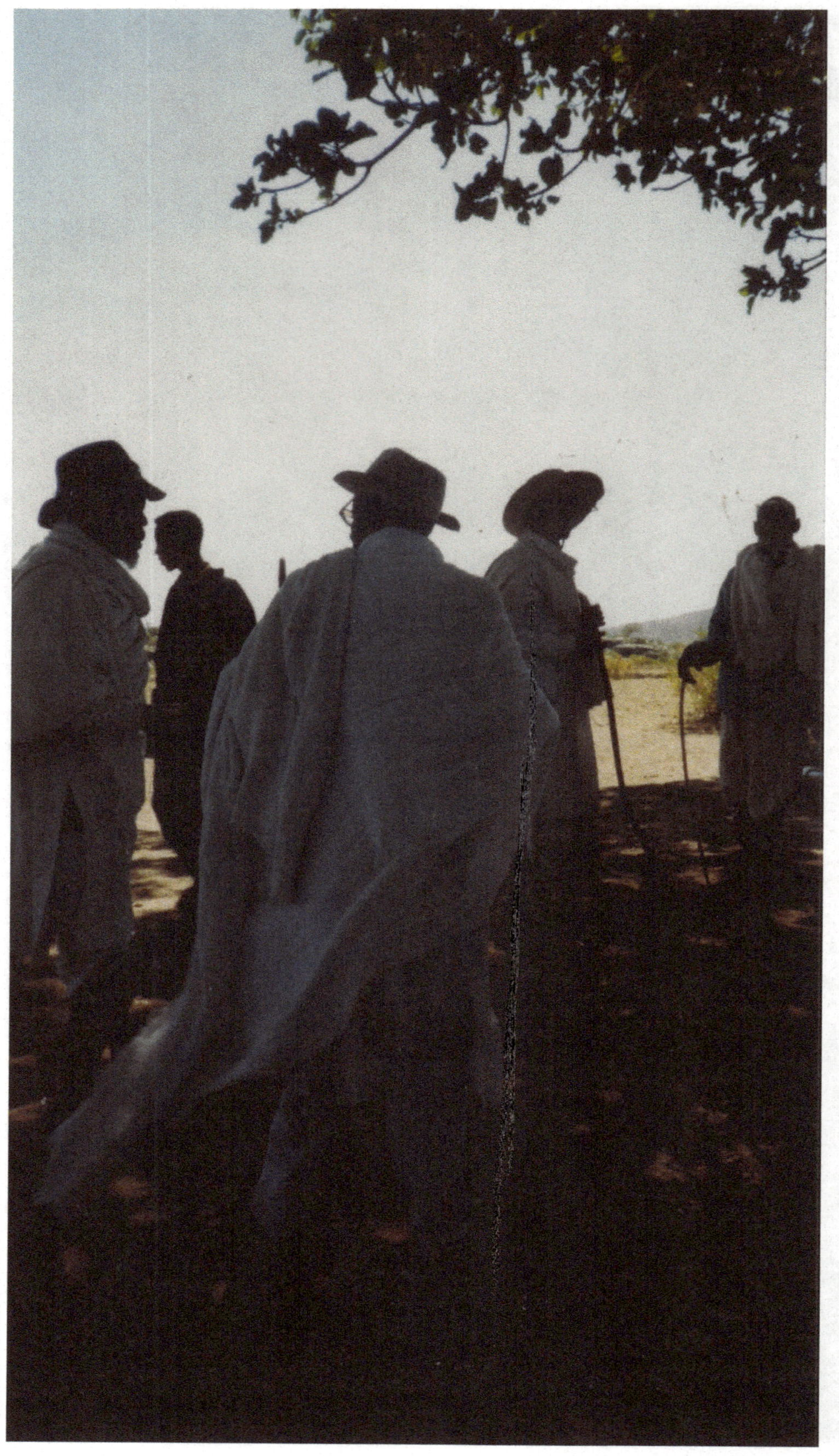

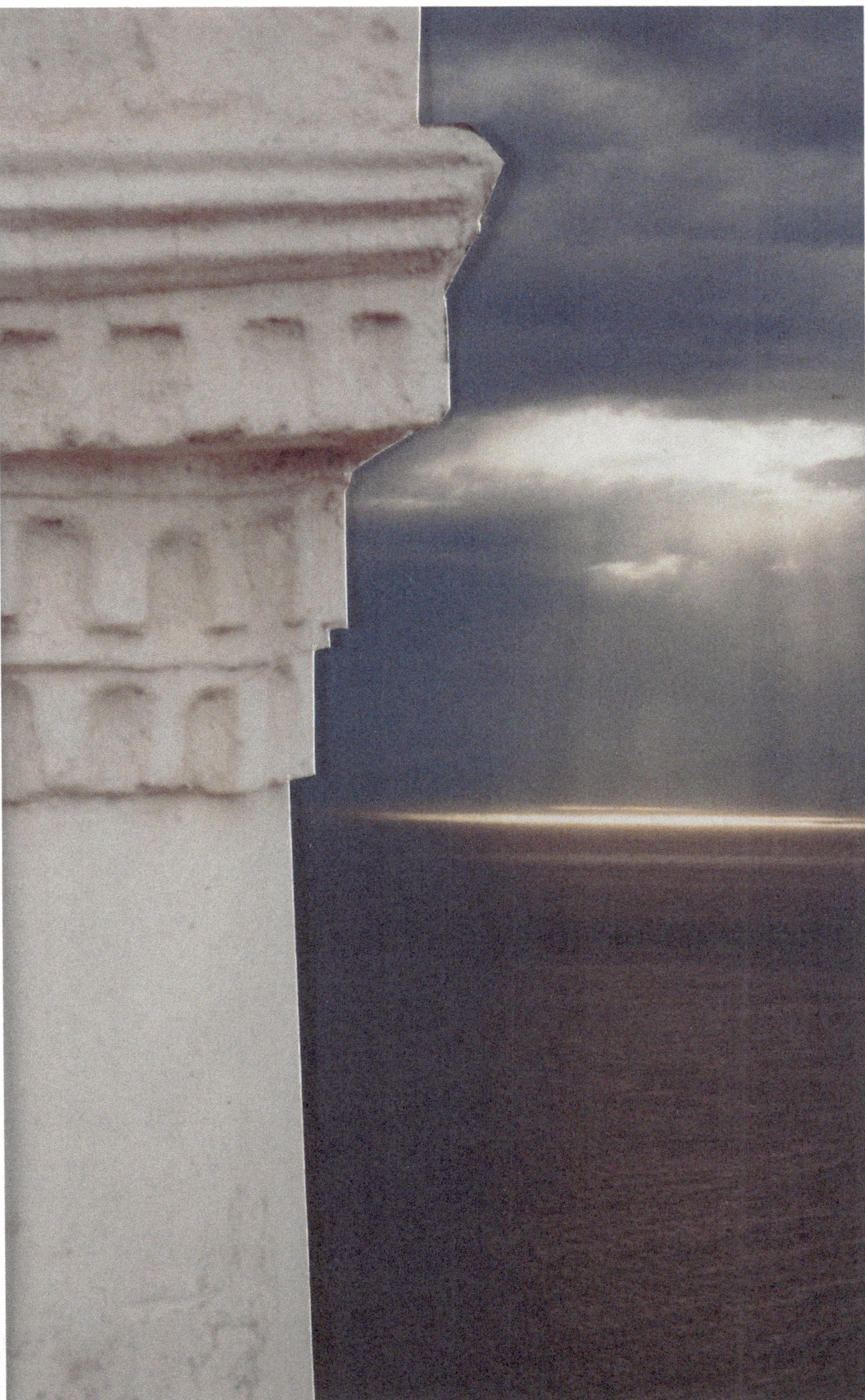

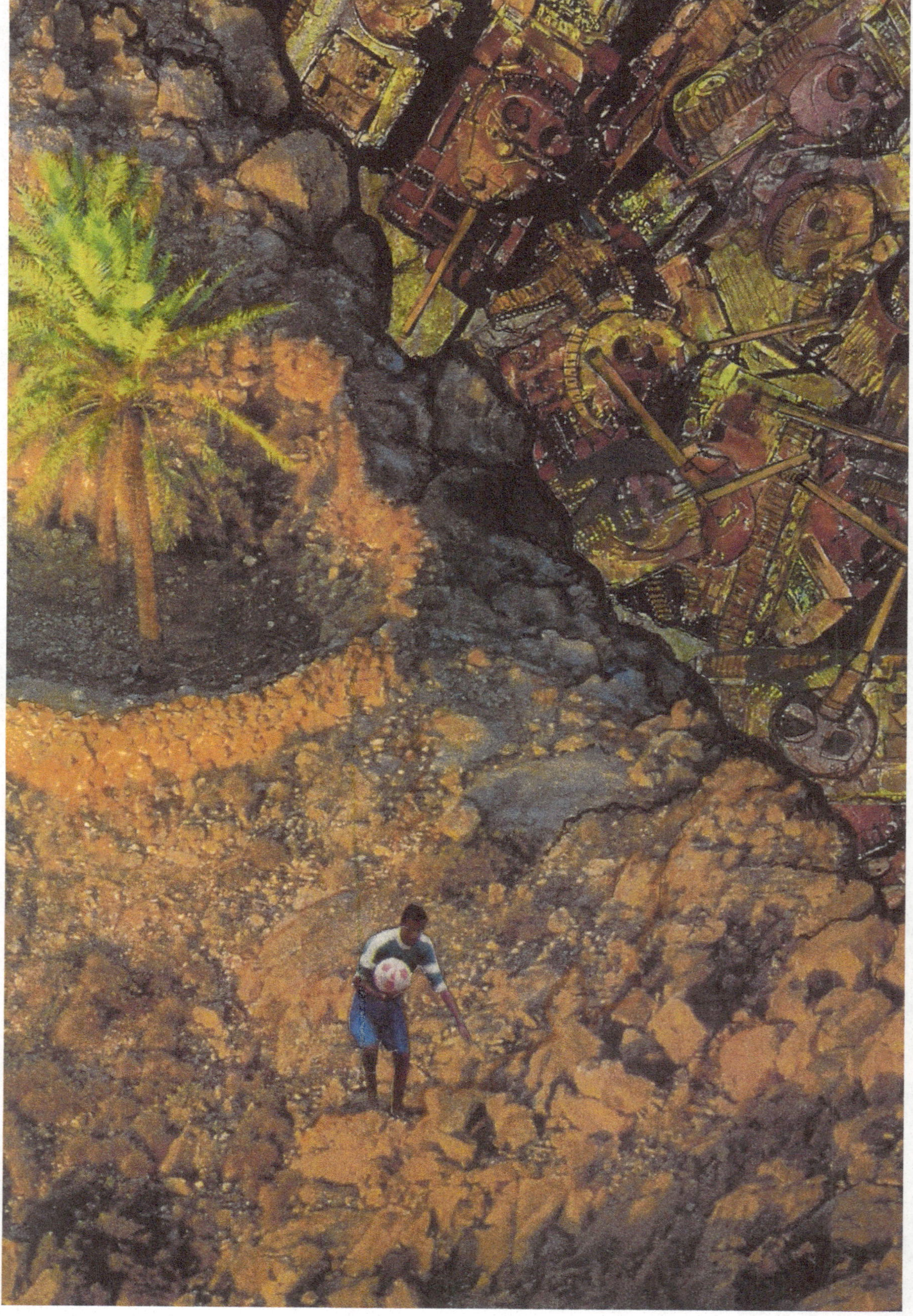

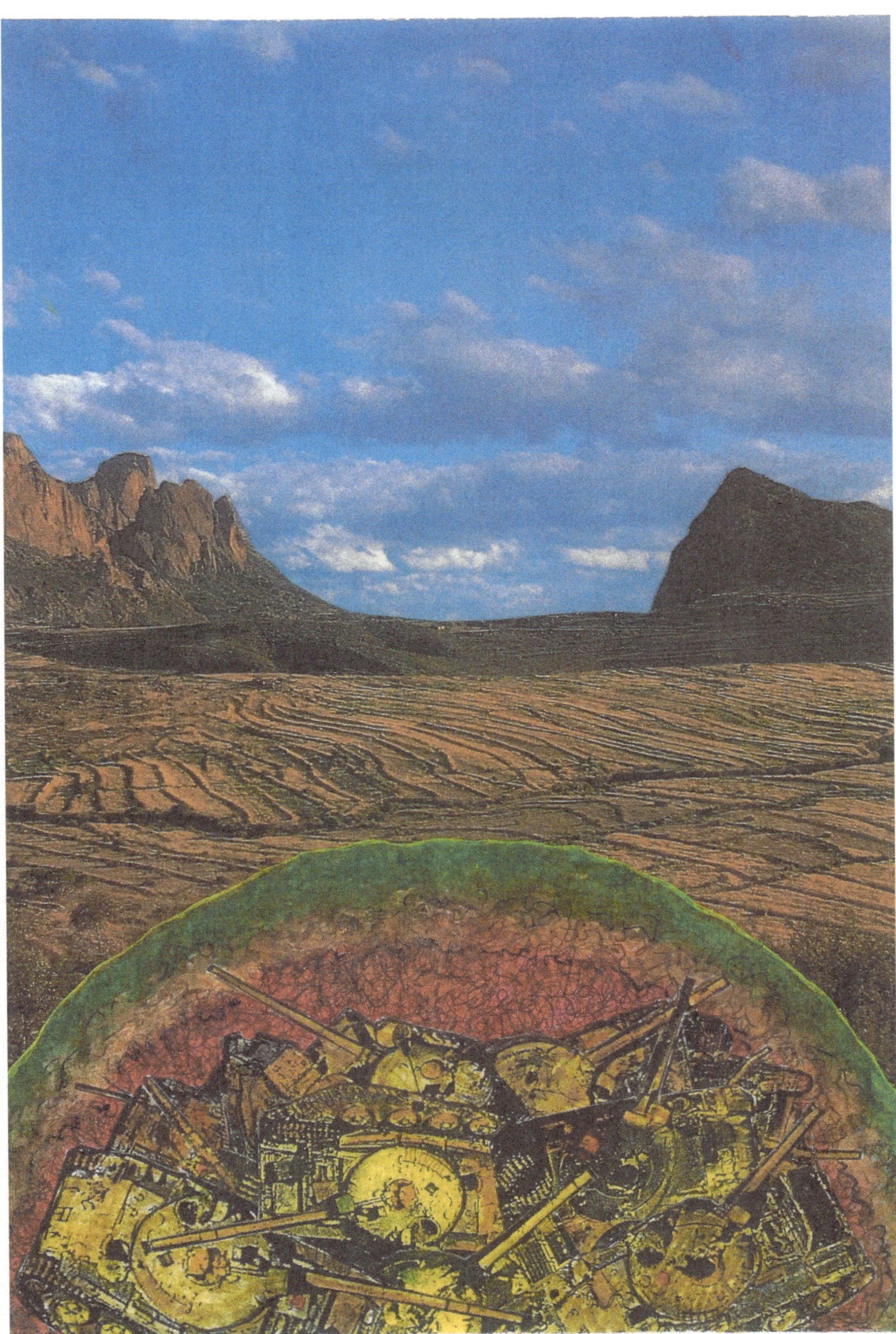

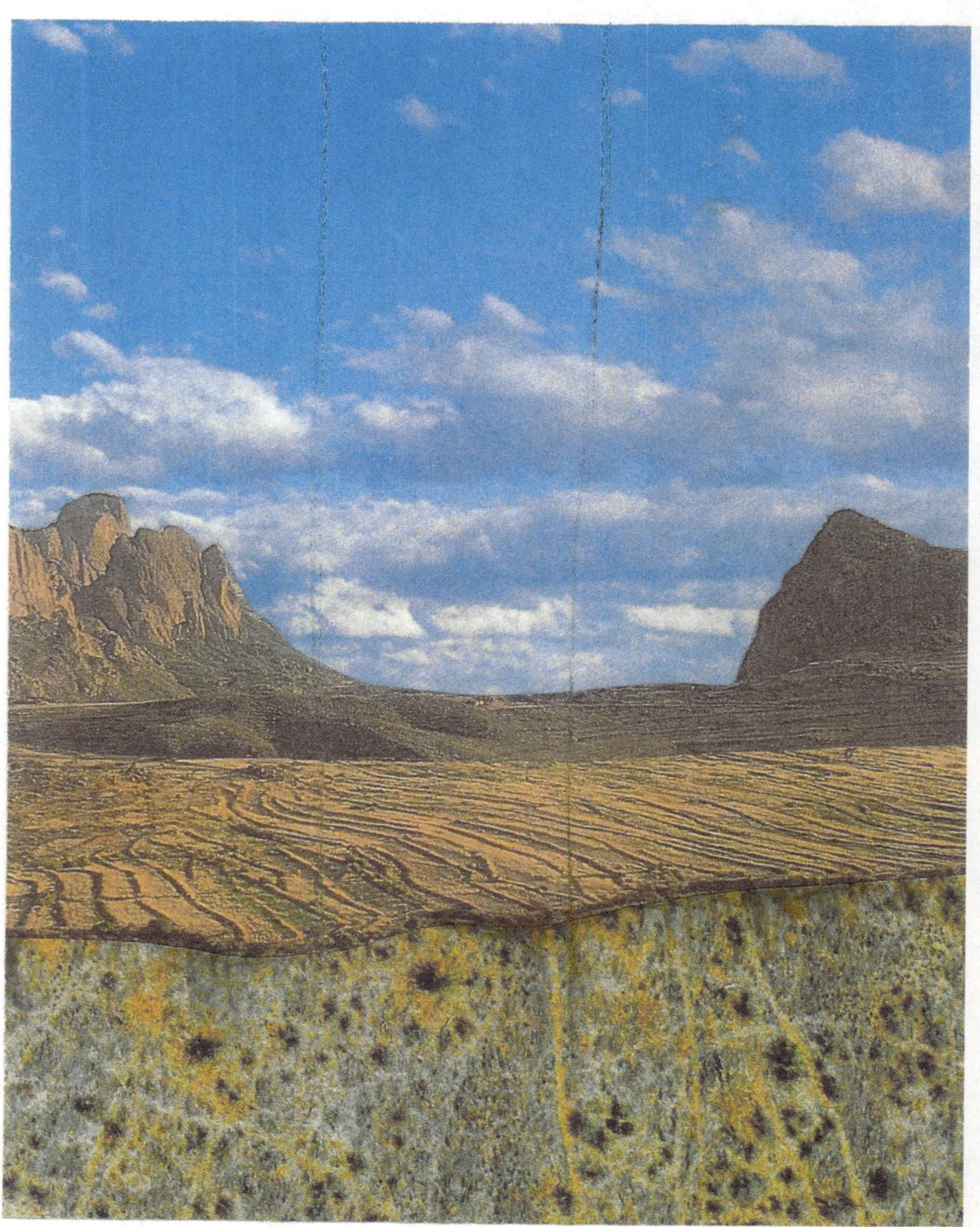

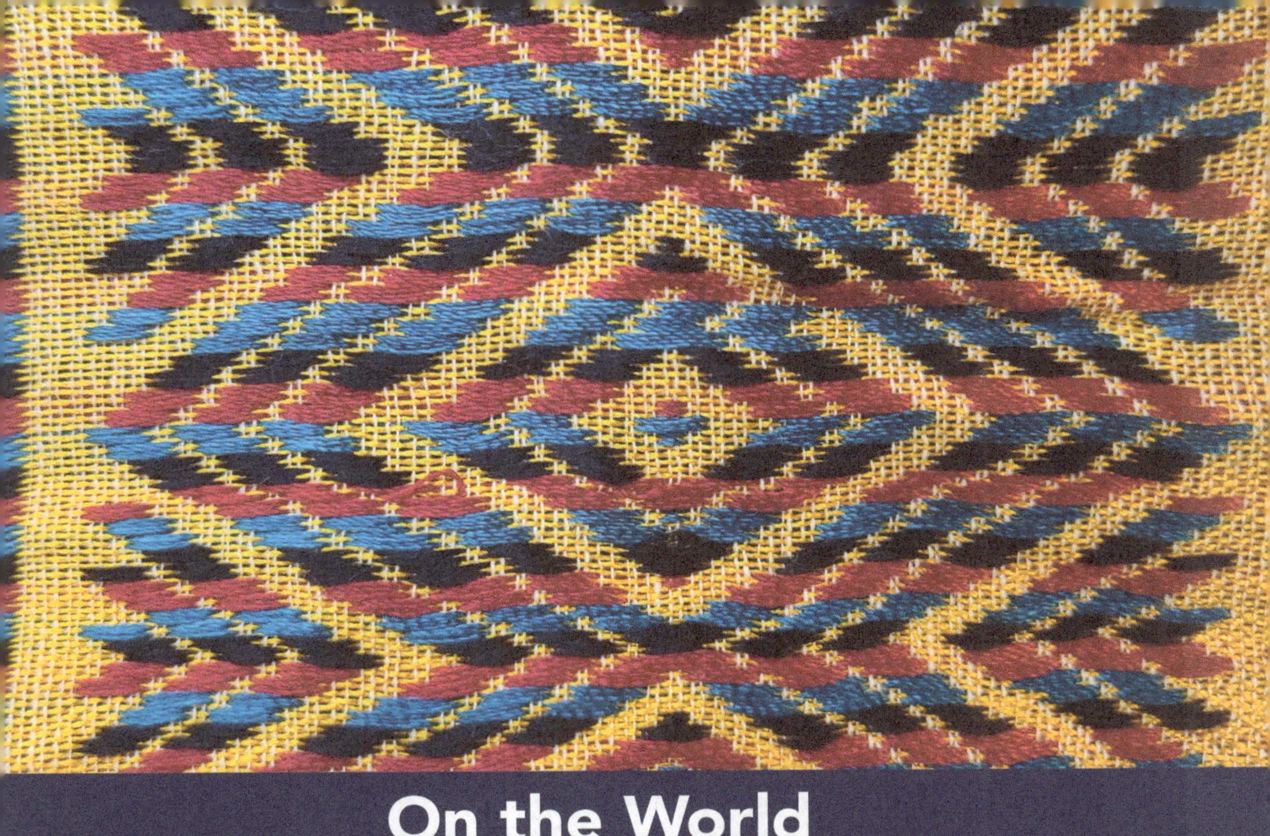

On the World

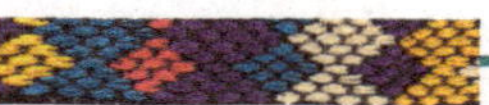

…For the occasion not existential or comprehensive.
If this were music, it would be chamber and not symphonic;
Or like a form of faith being knowledge purely visual,
Whether it's substance or not or evidence of anything
Other than some kind of story untold still to be assured
Endlessly through its allure…

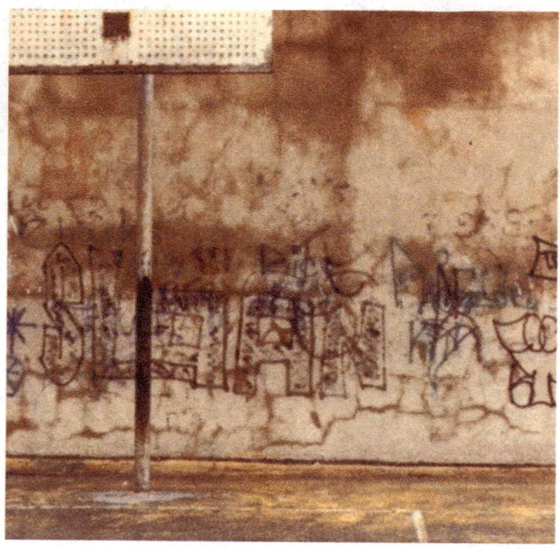

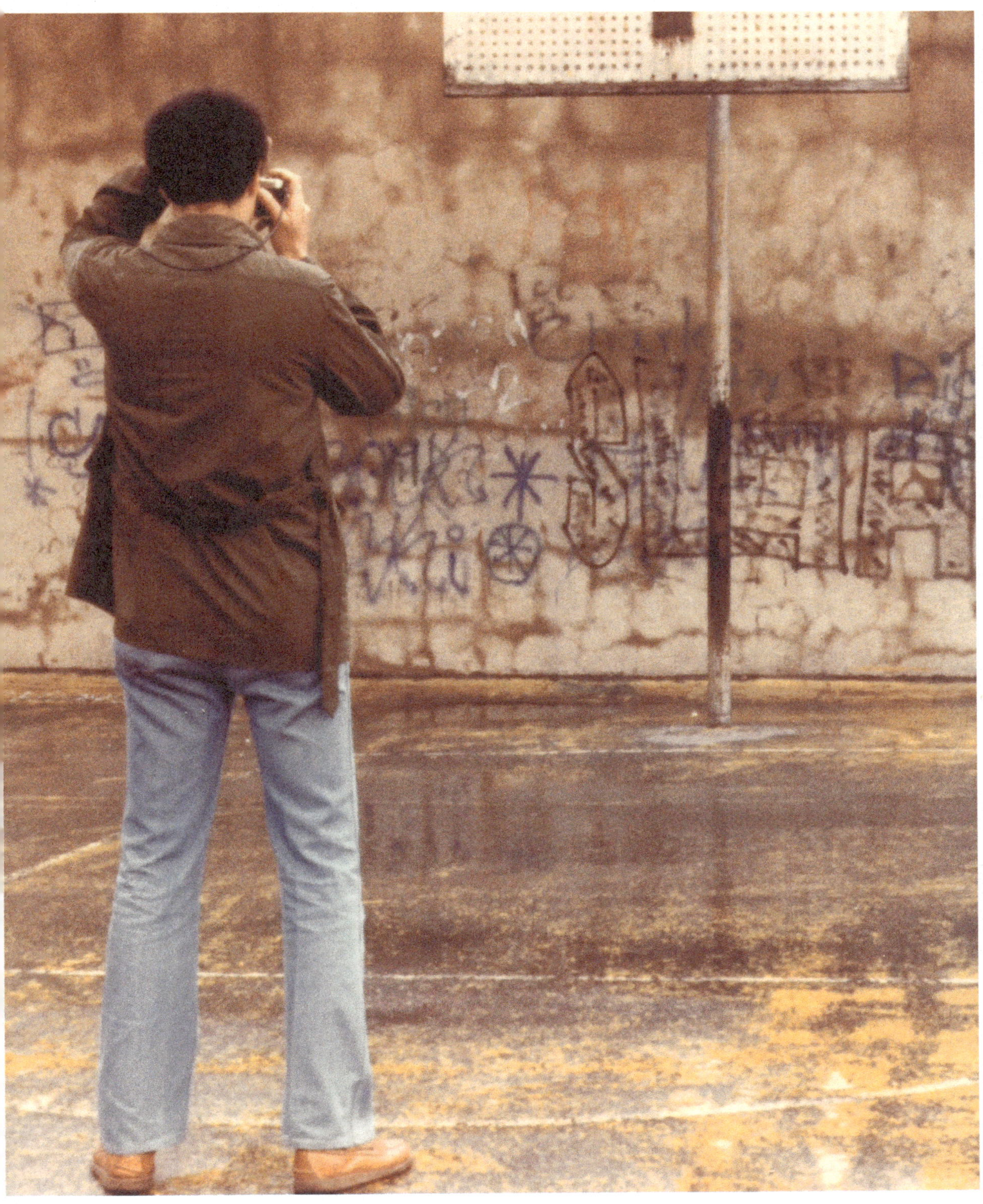

Head shots of both of us: sharp, clear, and reflective black and white;
Head shots of both of us: sharp, clear, and reflective black and white;
As we responded to what each other said: not monologue –
Dialogue in the tilt of a head, a determined parting
Or a quick tightening of the lips, a smile, a furrowing
Brow, and the shadows around somebody's eyes closing to think.

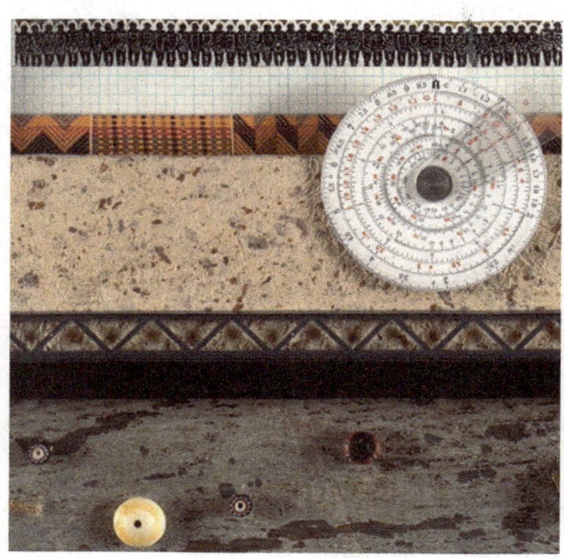

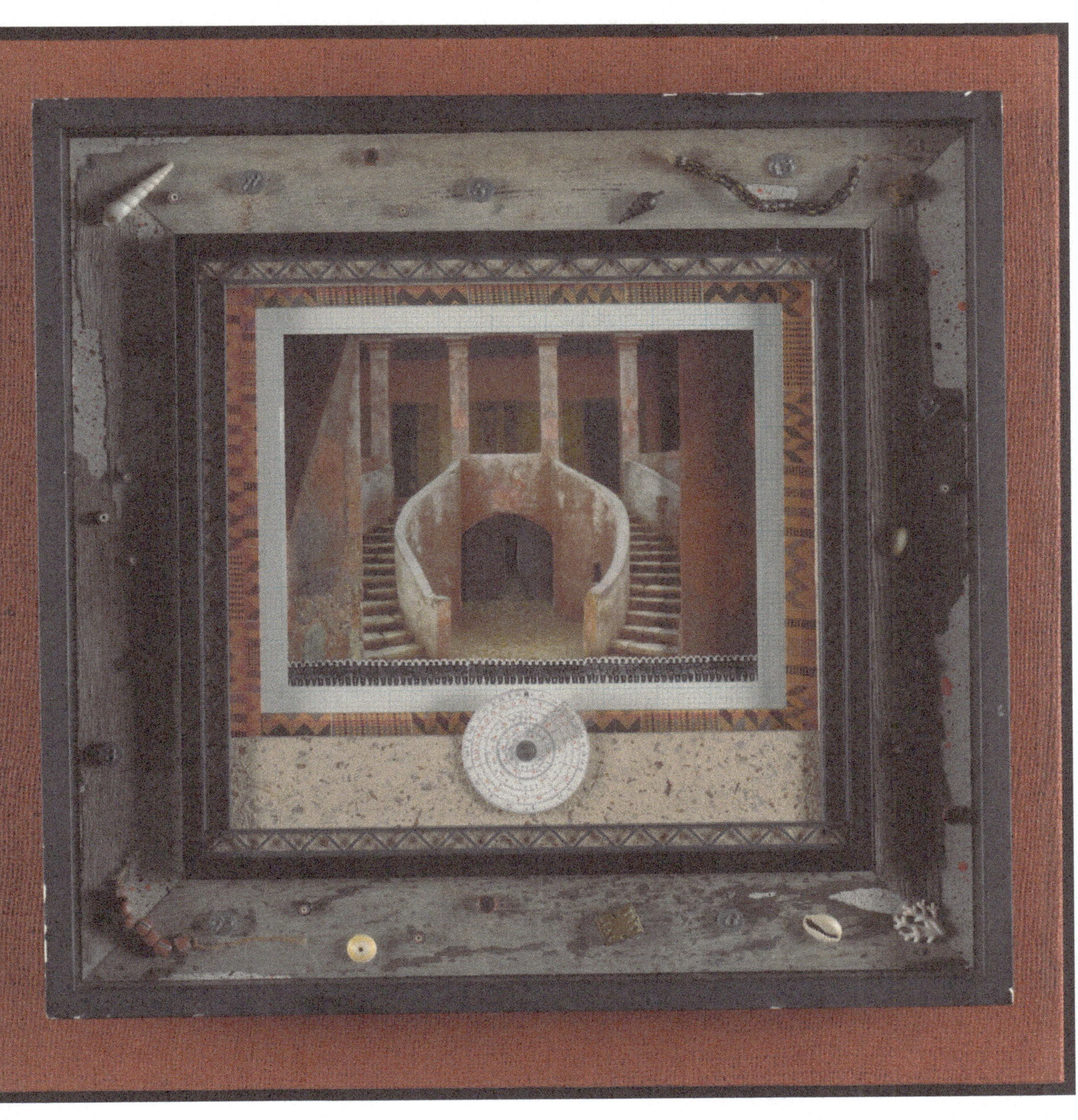

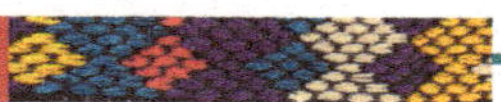

"It's a political minefield. If you think you can get through,
Why not try, when maybe no one else can. So, you must go back.
This is a part of the story you'll be missing all your life
If you don't."

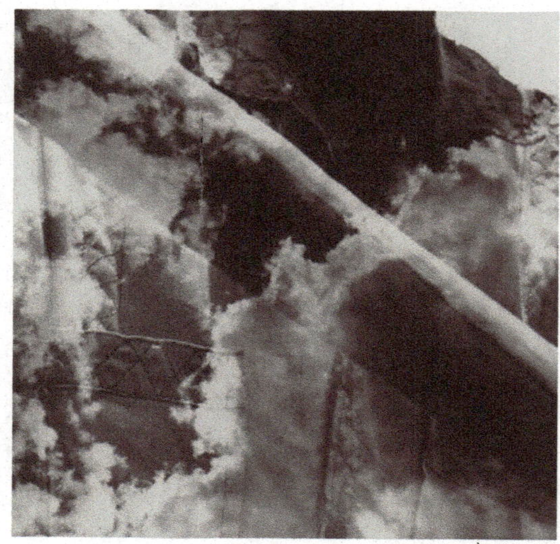

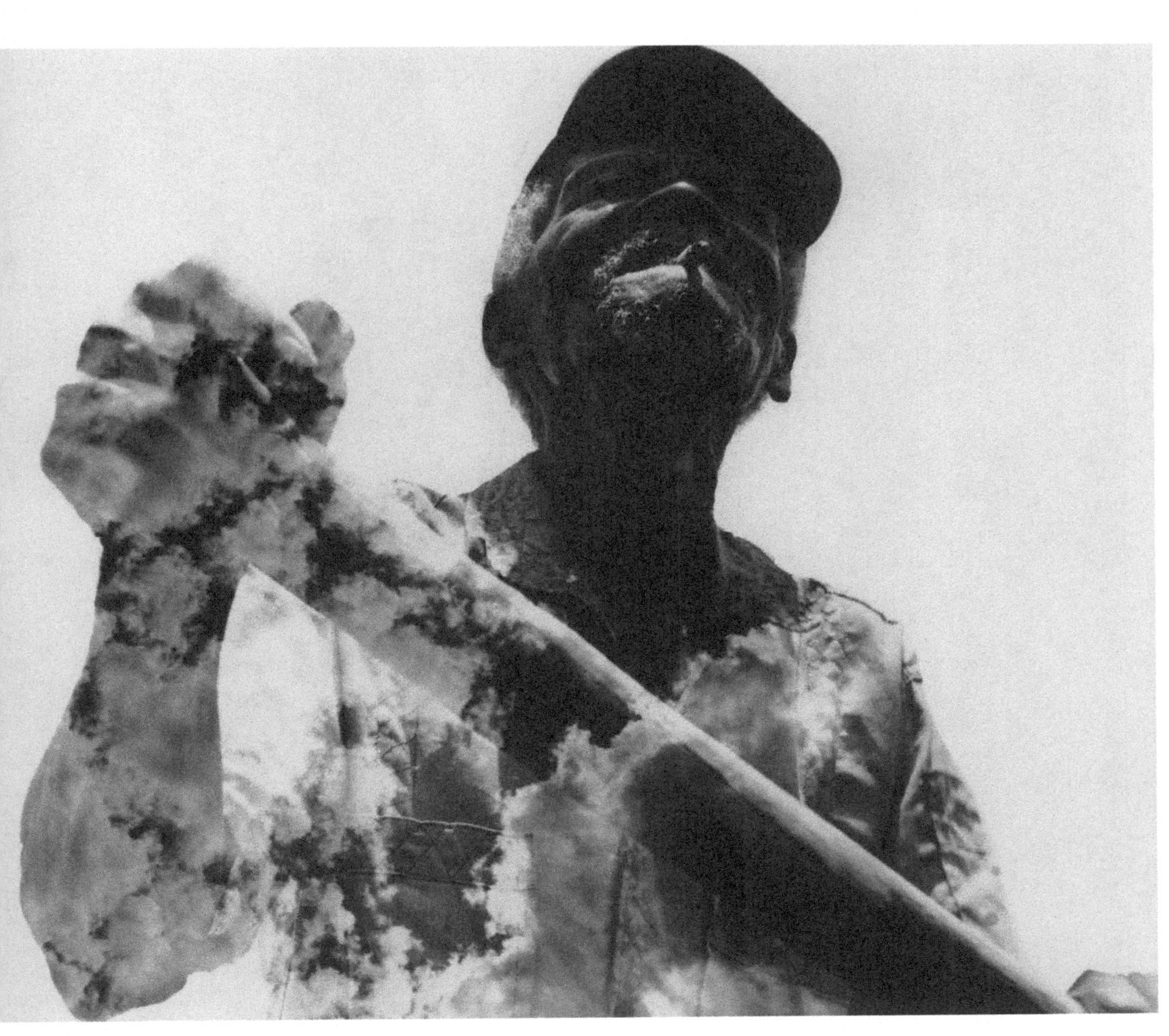

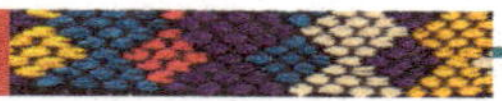

Roots run so deep and can wander in so many directions....

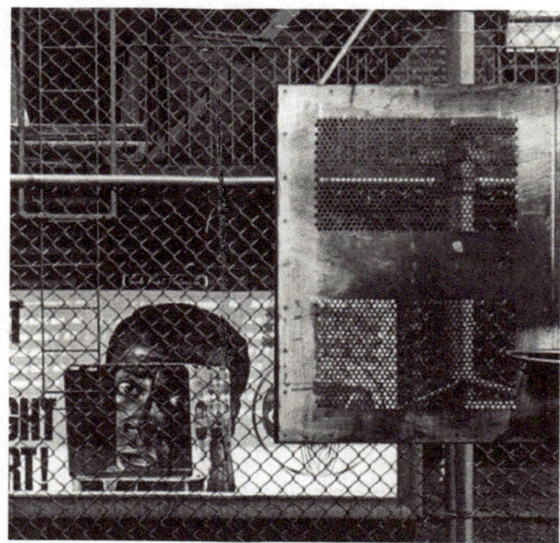

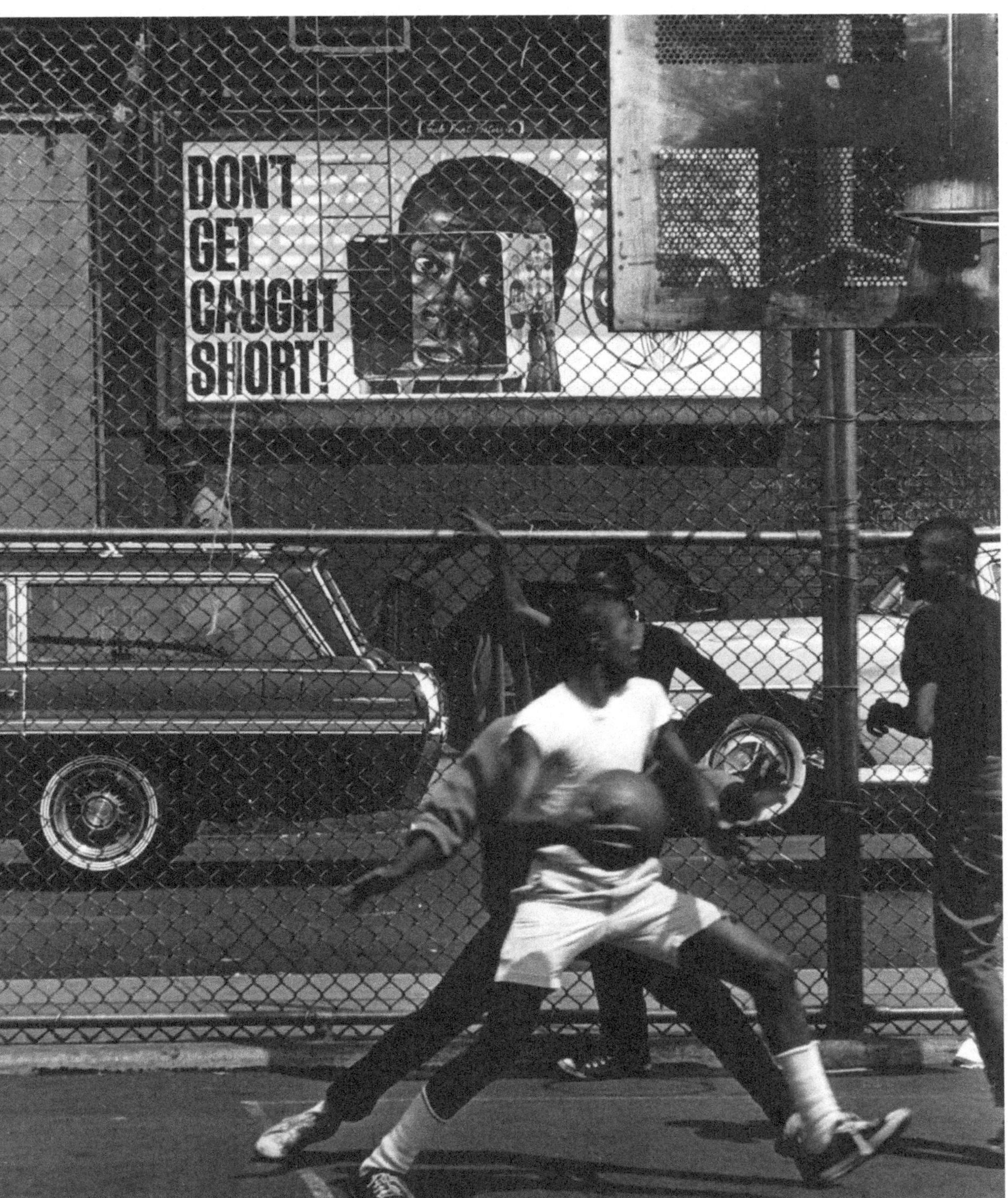

DON'T
GET
CAUGHT
SHORT!

Red like the clay of the Serengeti when it's splashed with blood.

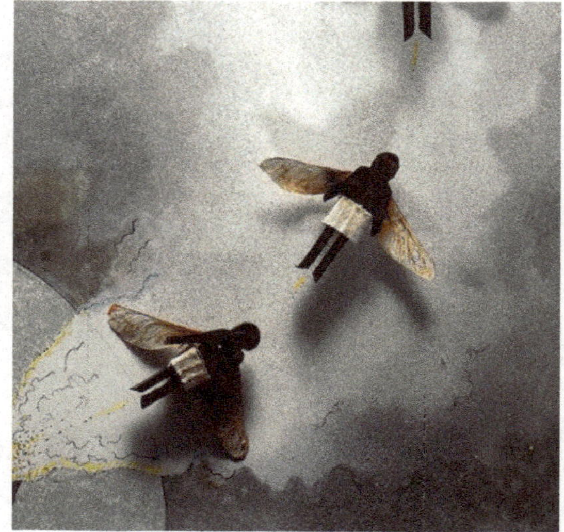

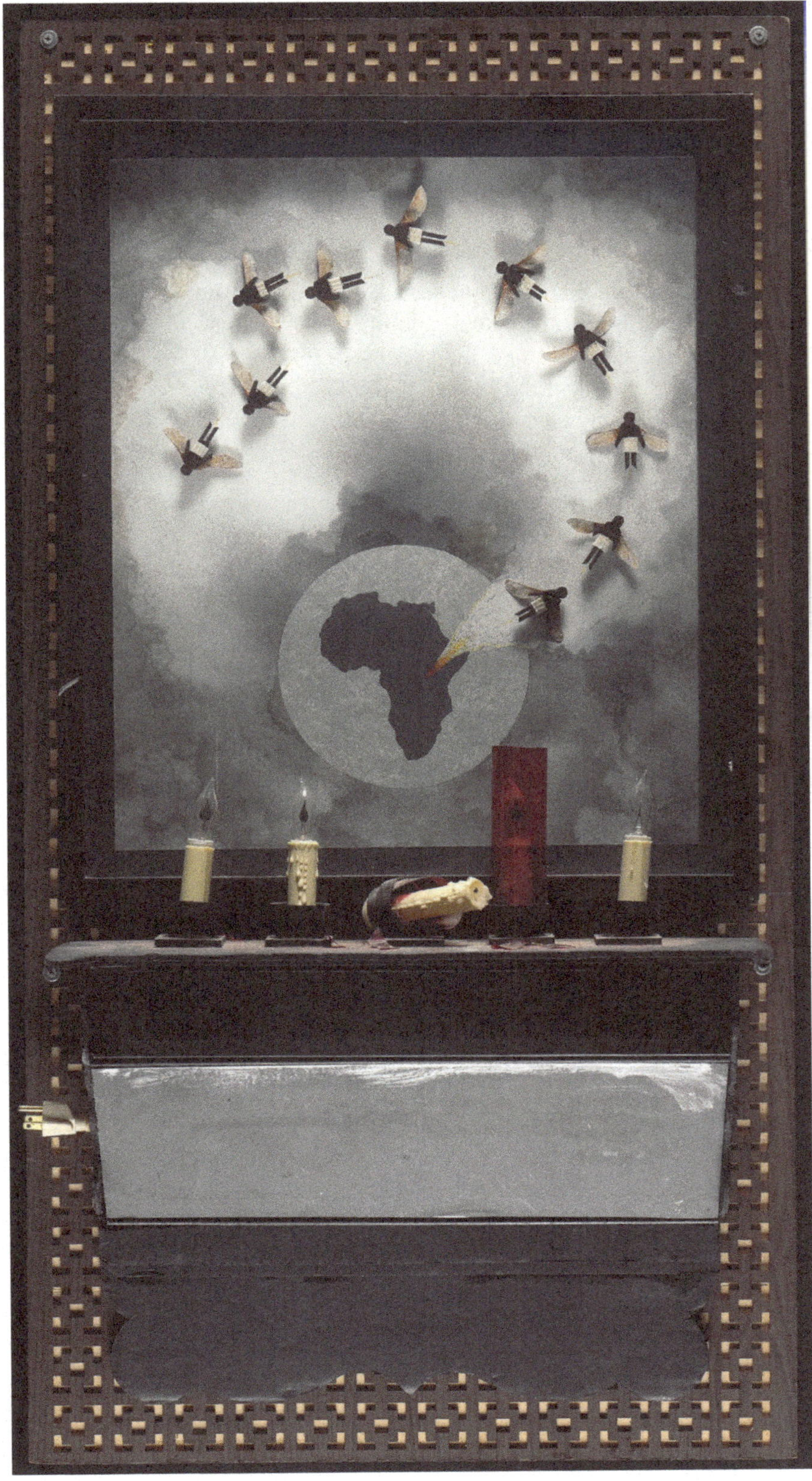

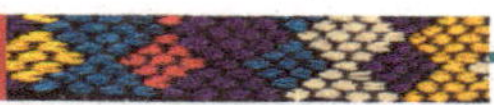

...Sykes identified
With a place to the point that it all but seemed like he was home
Through a spontaneous kind of visual tapping into
Places with histories strewn across their surfaces set deep
In counter histories' layers of the broken and intact
Constantly moving among each other....

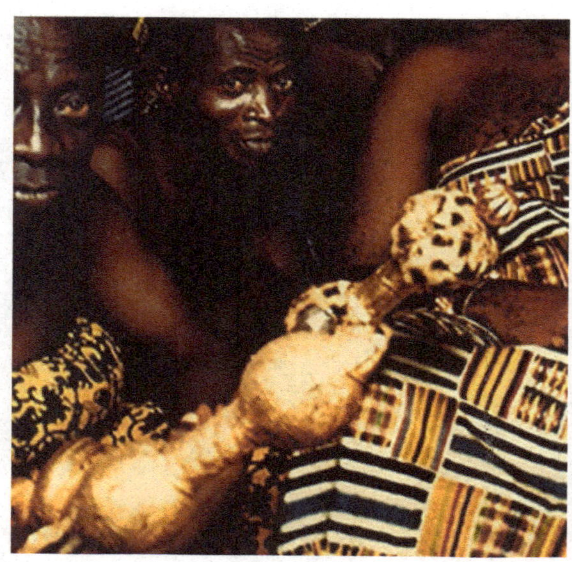

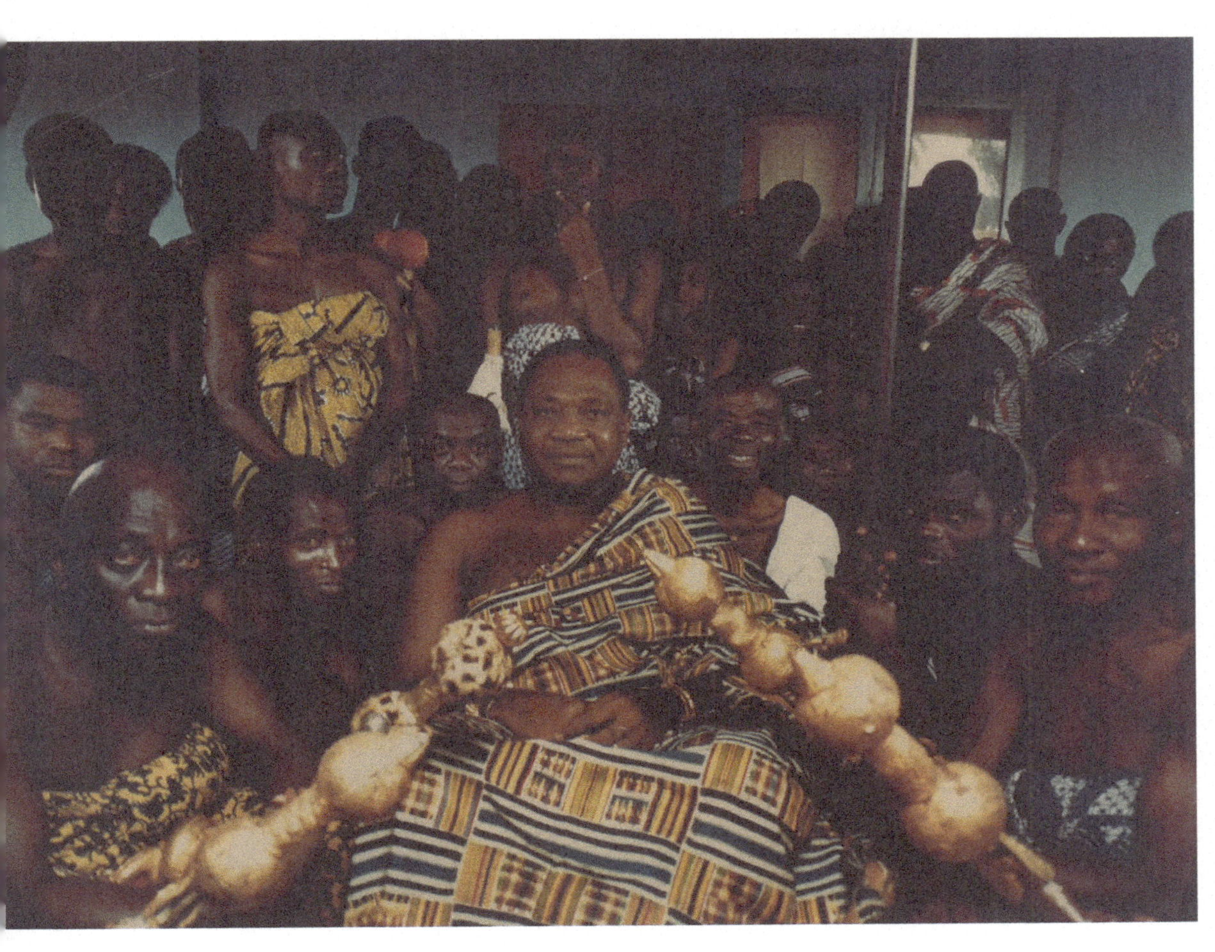

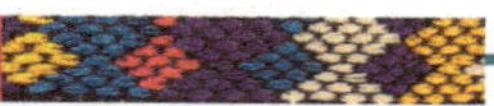

Who was he? I can remember Barbara once telling me
Only half joking and lovingly: that "tall quiet black man
With short hair, wearing an overcoat, and taking a picture
Of himself in black and white reflected in a store window."

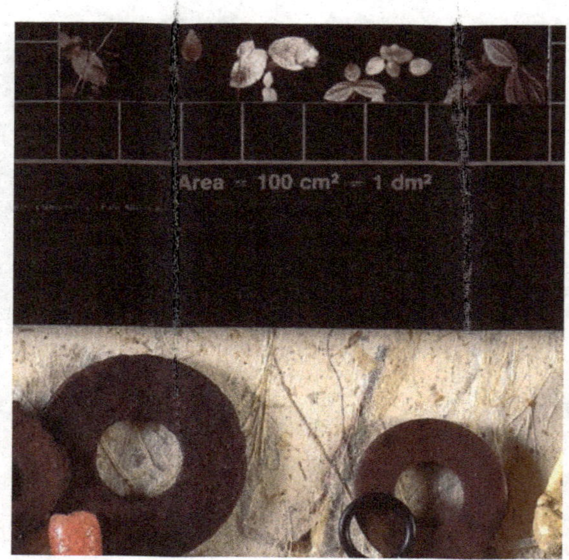

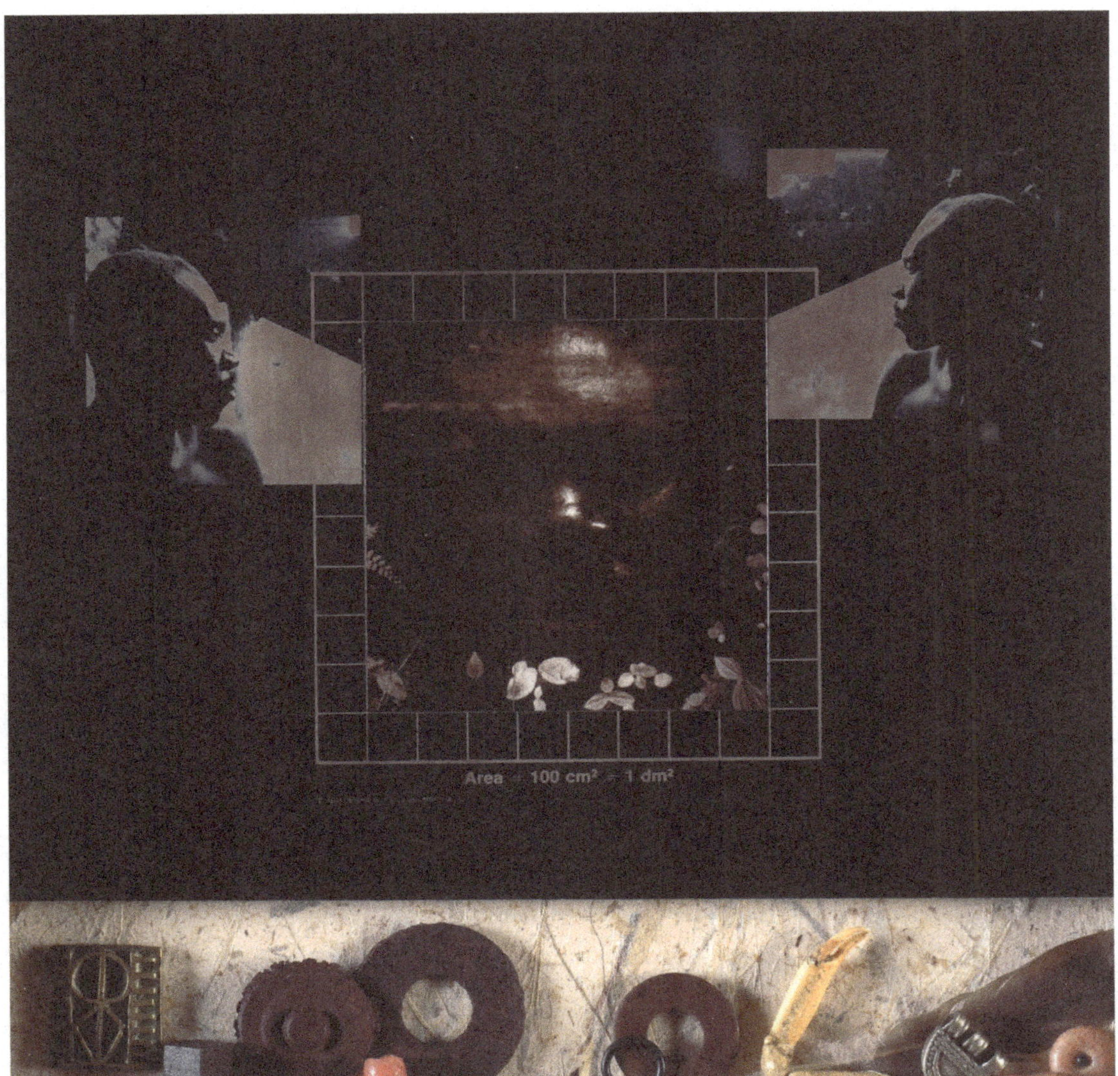

Area = 100 cm² = 1 dm²

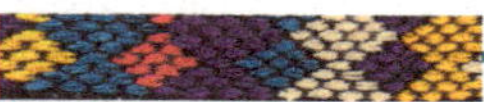

When I would tell him of beautiful or challenging moments
During the trip, he'd say, "Cantalupo, you like it too much."

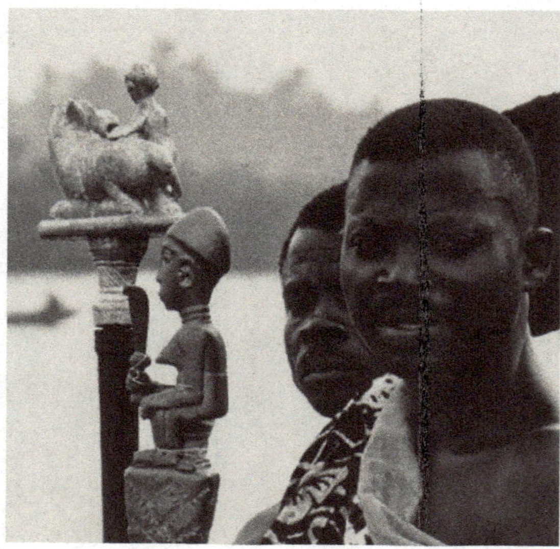

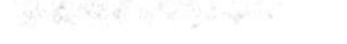

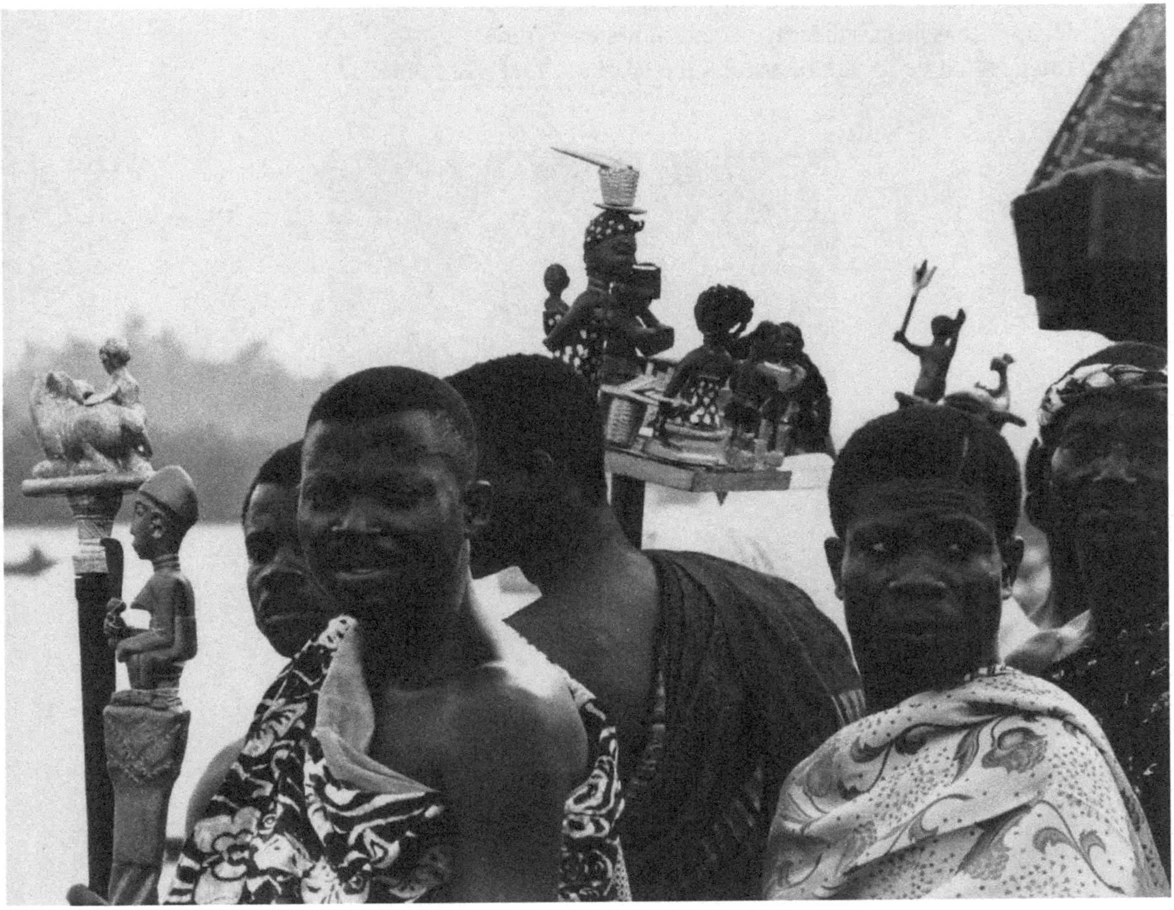

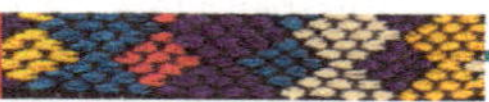

History was Sykes's heartbeat first and then the heartbeat of
History that he saw deeply rooted in the everyday
Images that he found all around the world to feel like home.

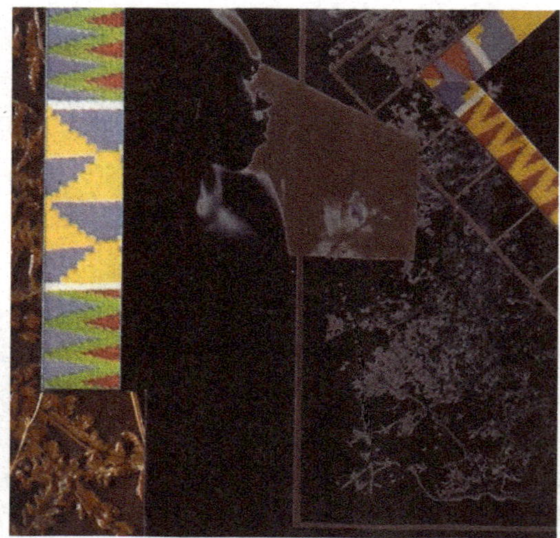

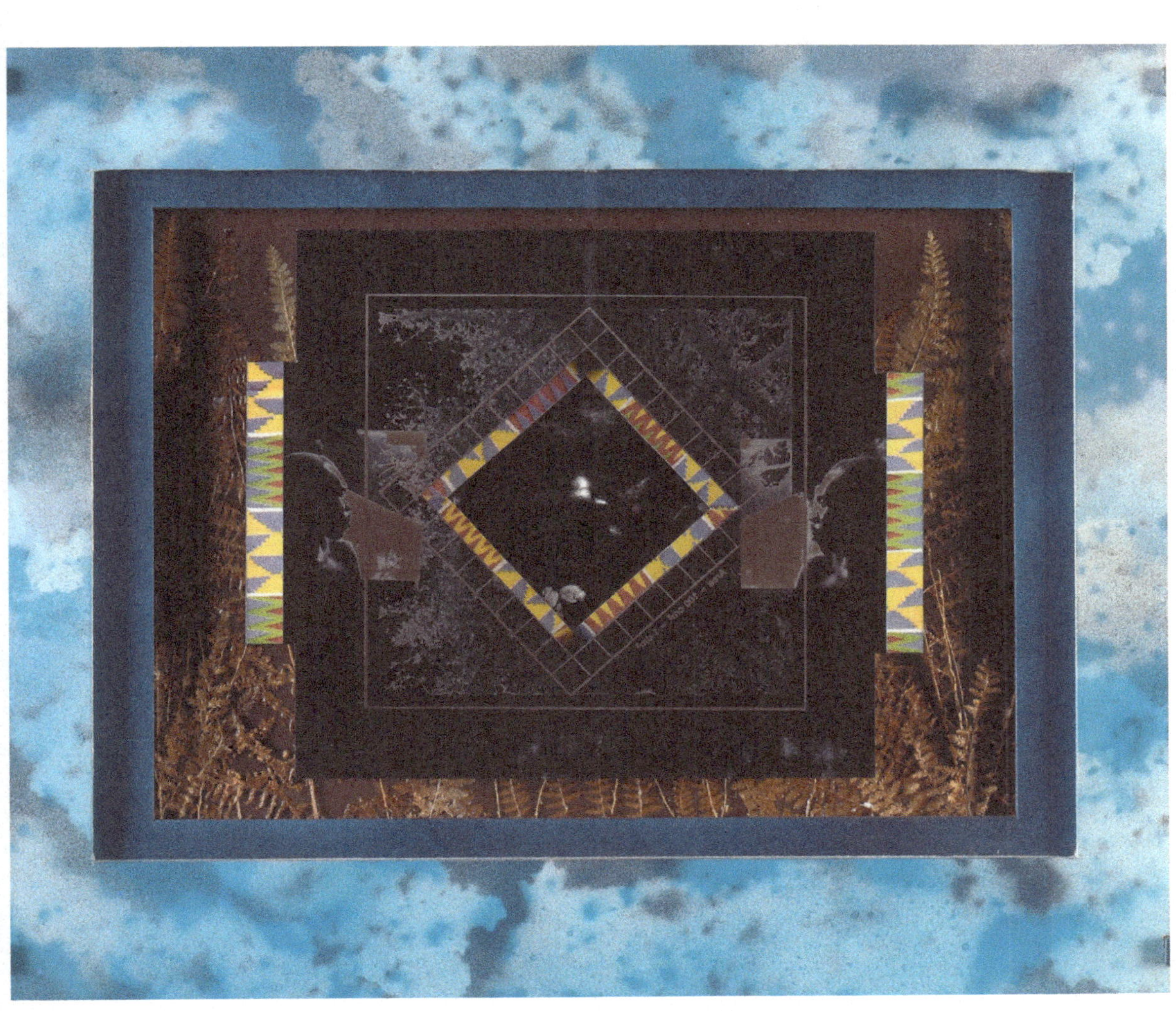

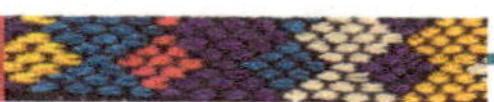

Not without knowing the shootings, clubbings, mass graves, detentions,
Genocide, pogroms, beheadings, bombings, torture, kidnappings,
Fevers, starvation, and war within these very same pictures.
All of it happened, they say. It isn't under the surface.
That's what the surface was made from here. What else would it look like?

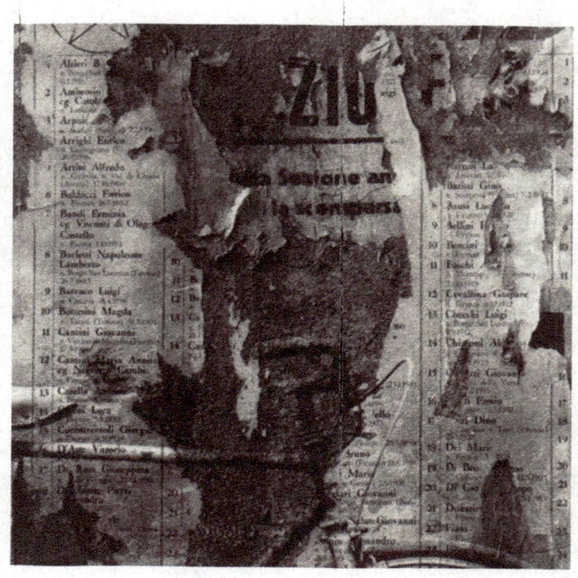

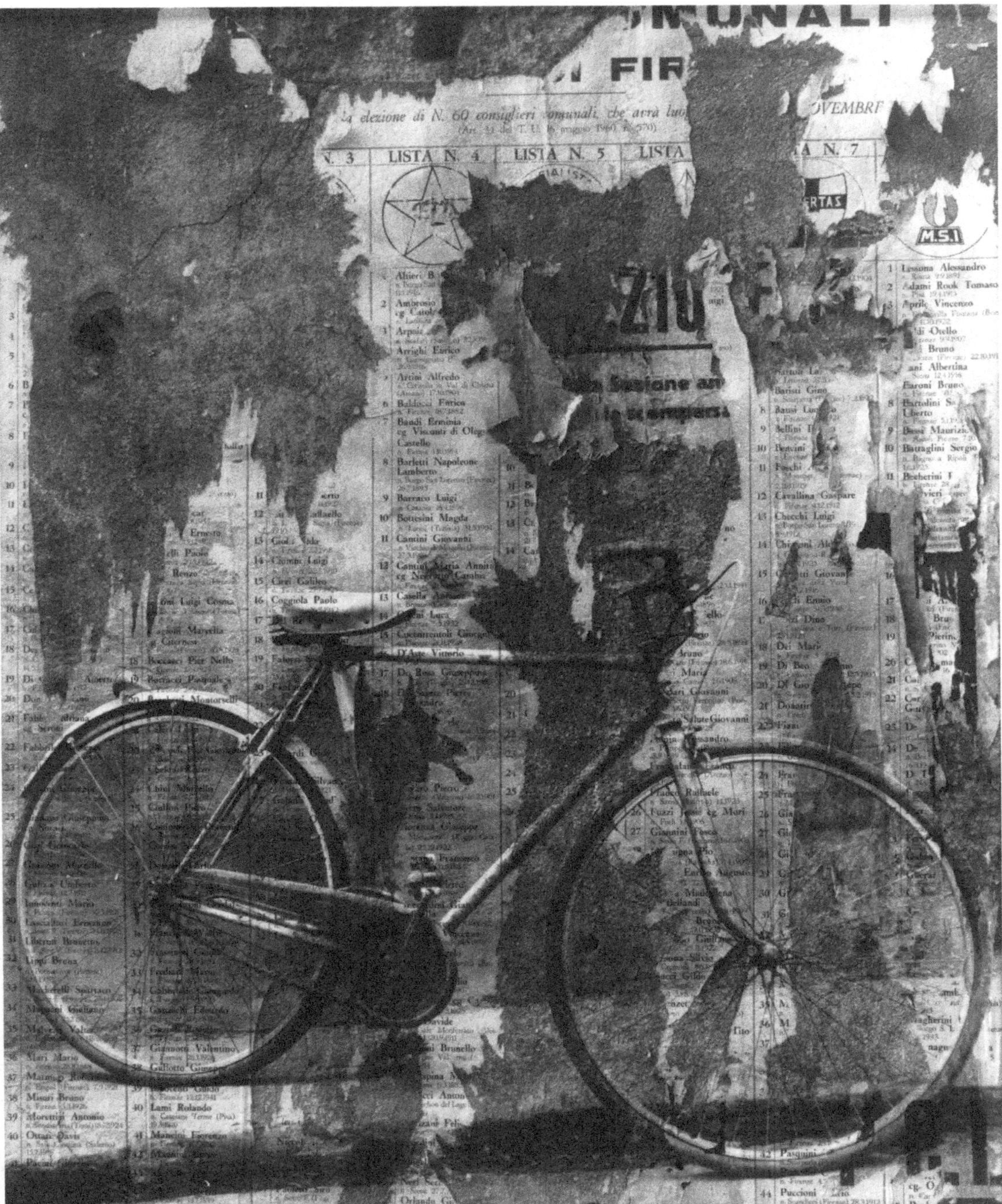

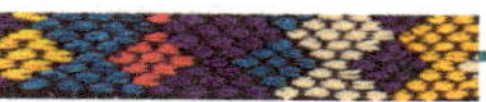

…history only went back
To Ellis Island, east twenty miles of Orange, New Jersey,
And a ship's manifest listing my grandfather's name, Carlo,
Ninety-nine years before, when he landed from Calabria.
What in my family came before that I have no idea.

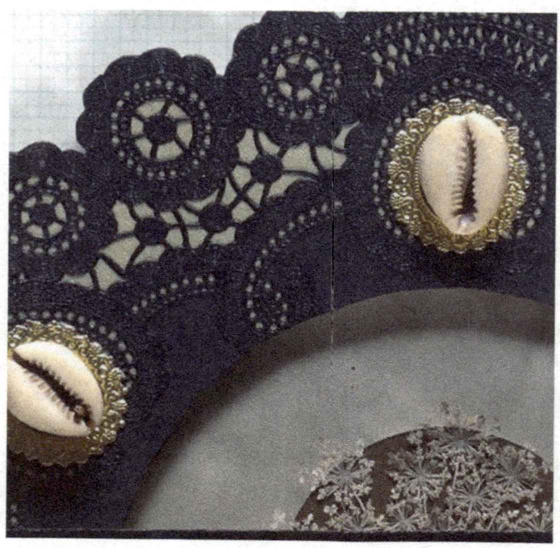

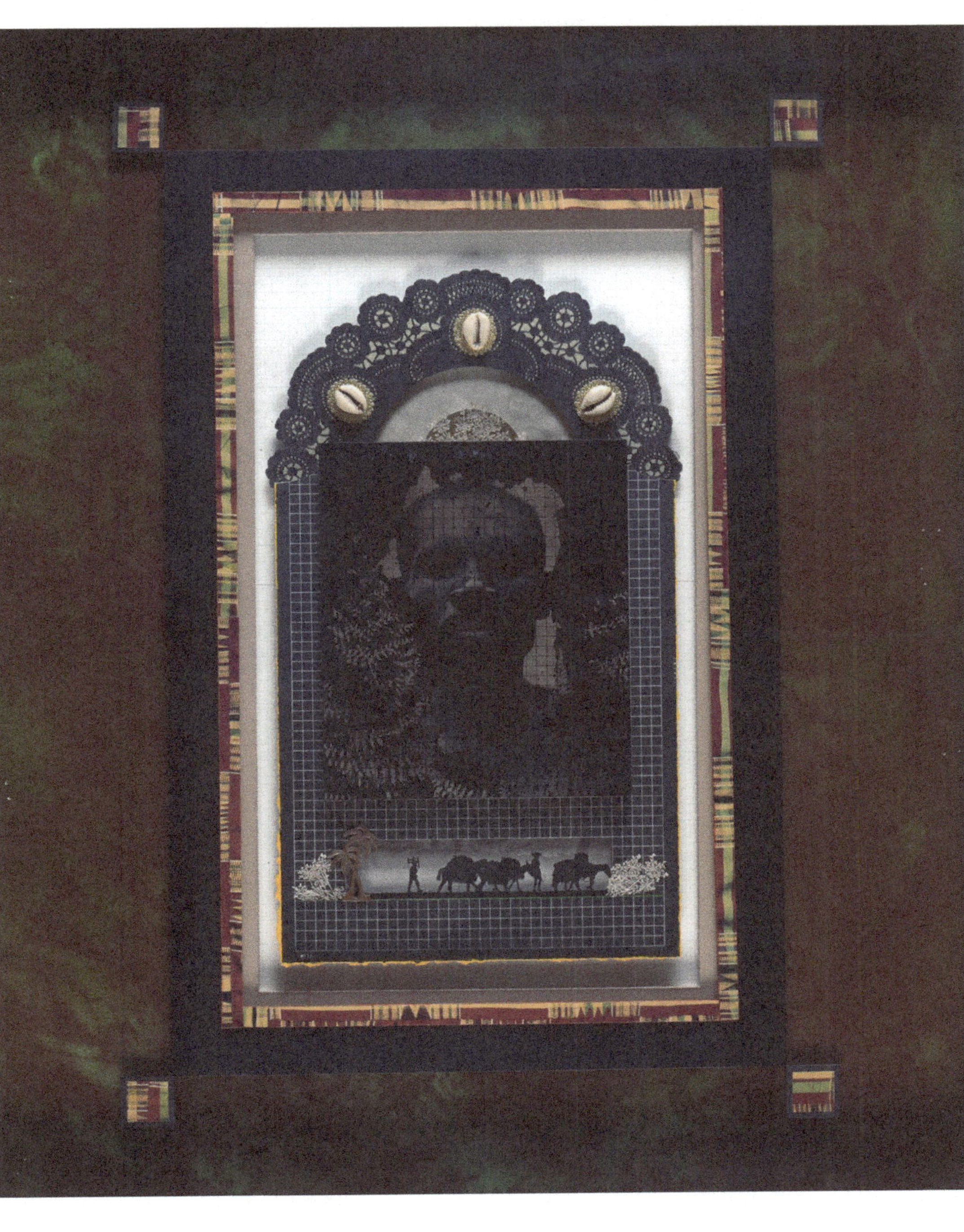

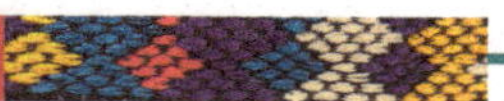

It seems abstract or like sunlight finally braking through damp grass;
It could be maps cut up into little pieces rearranged
Not by cartographers but by poets and philosophers.

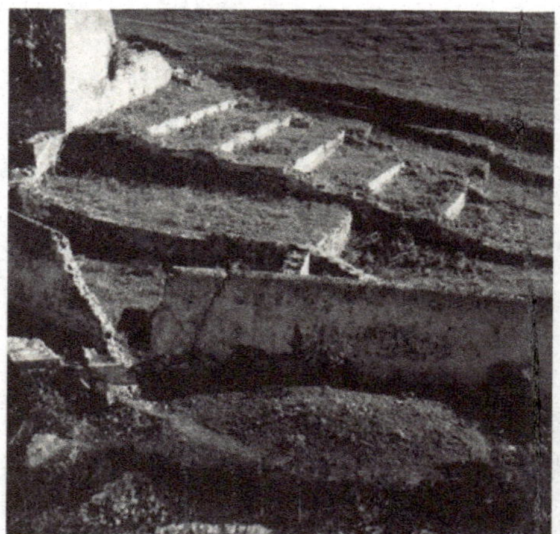 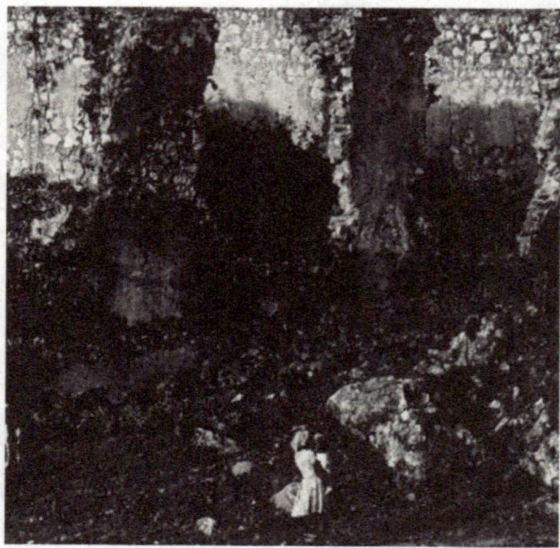

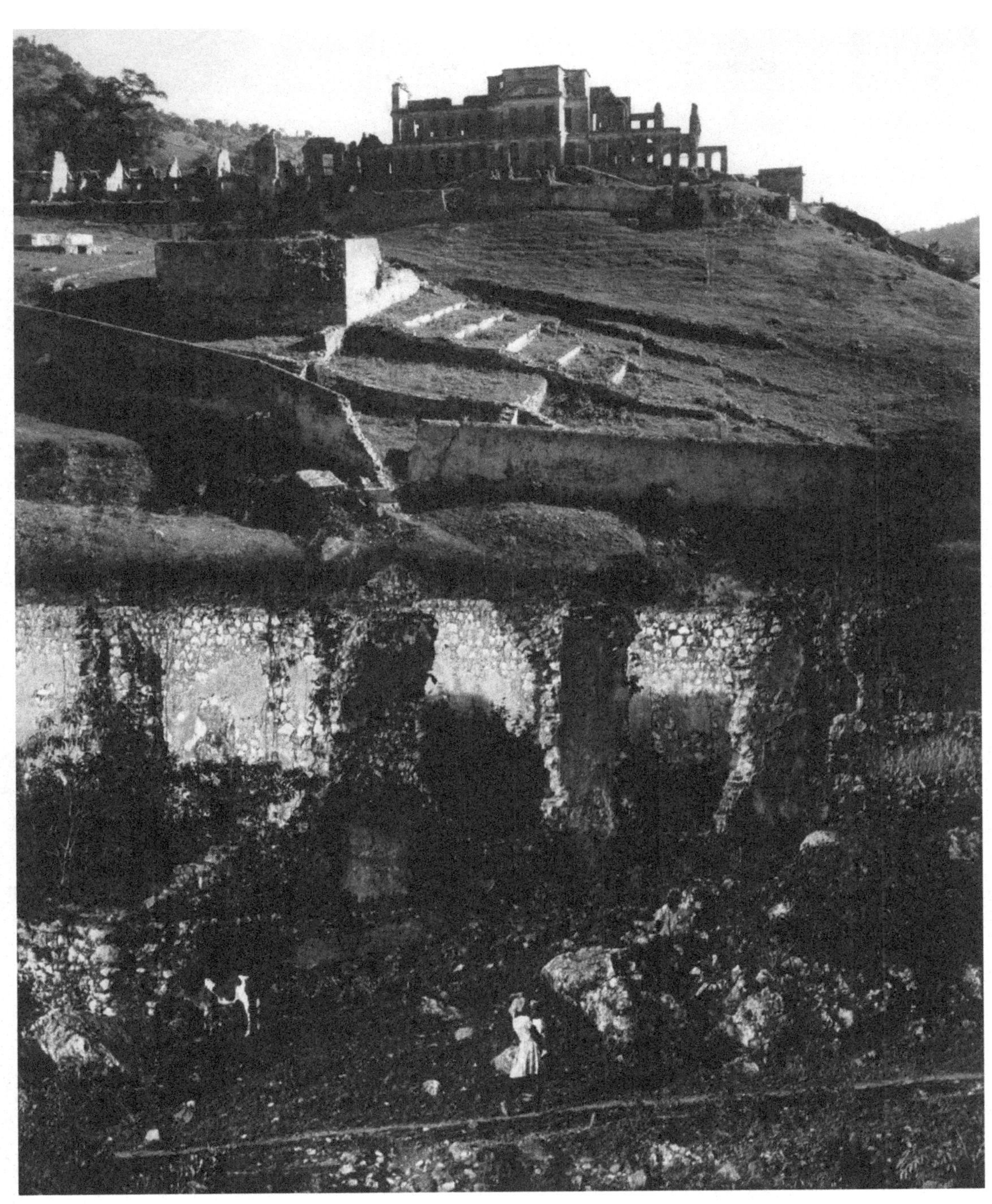

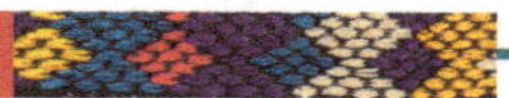

Sykes showed that I should be in that picture when I didn't know:

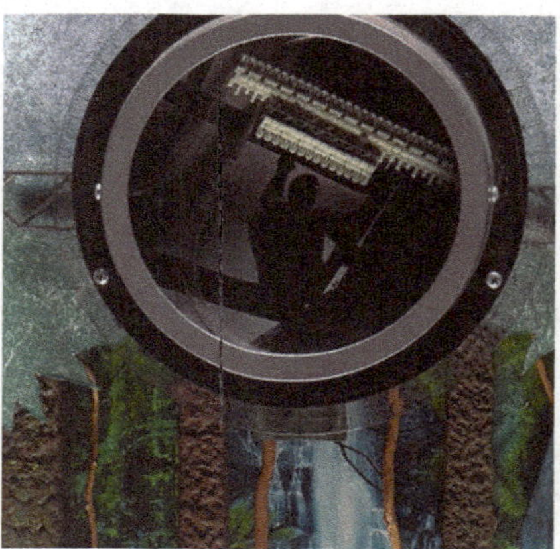

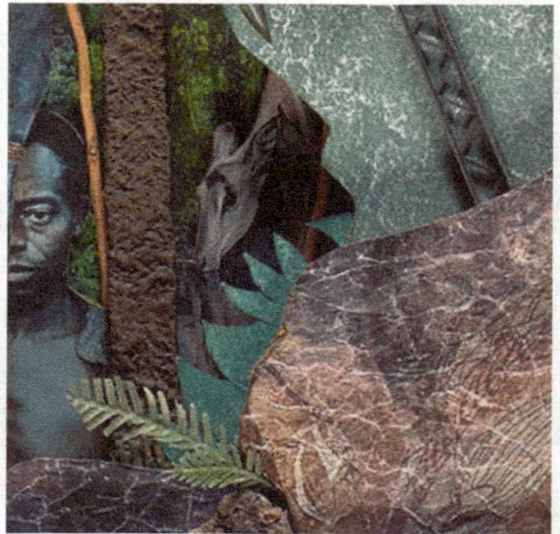

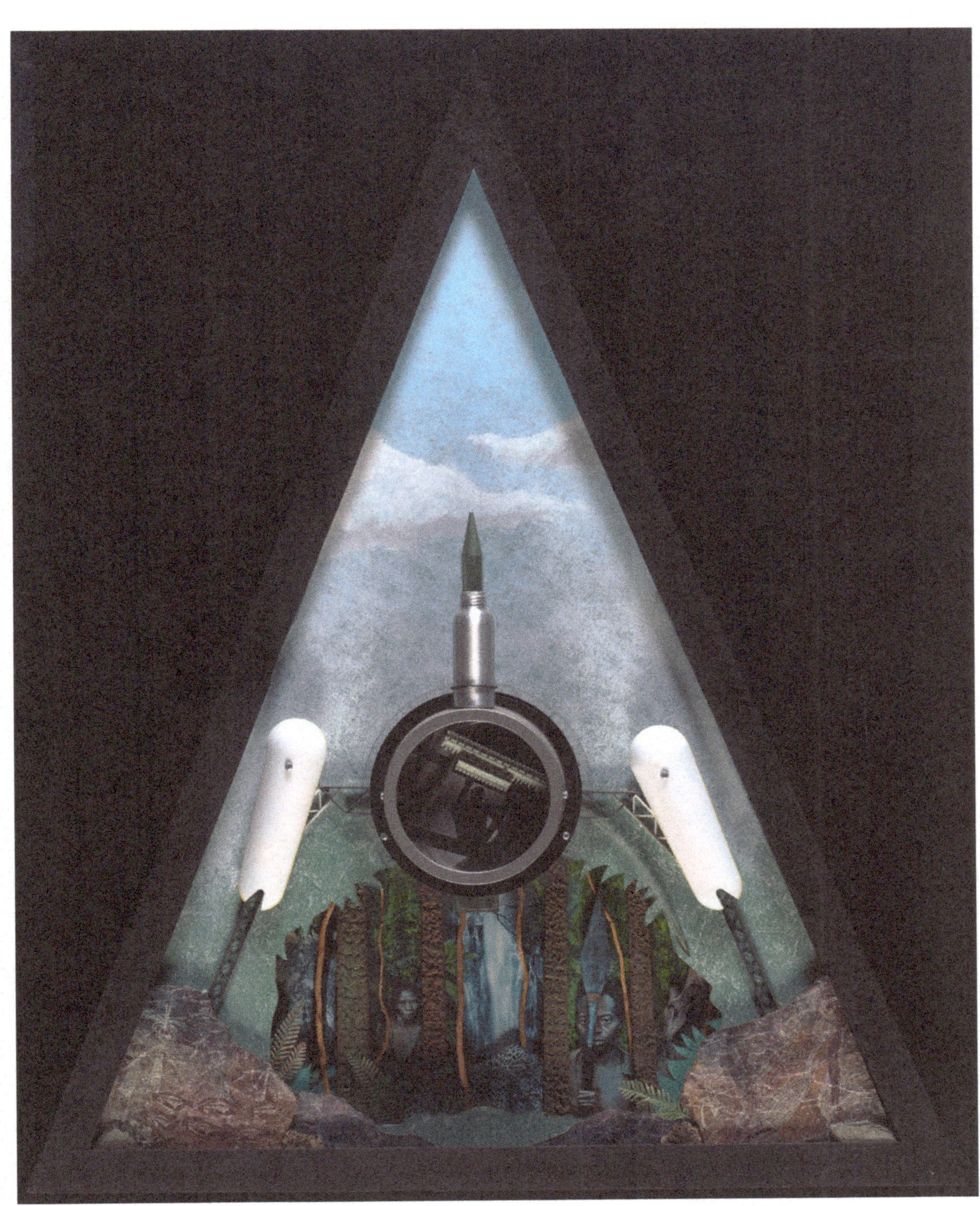

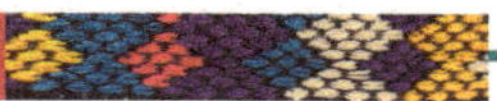

Sykes and I walking together traded images and words
Trying to join them together so that we could maybe see
How an epiphany happens....

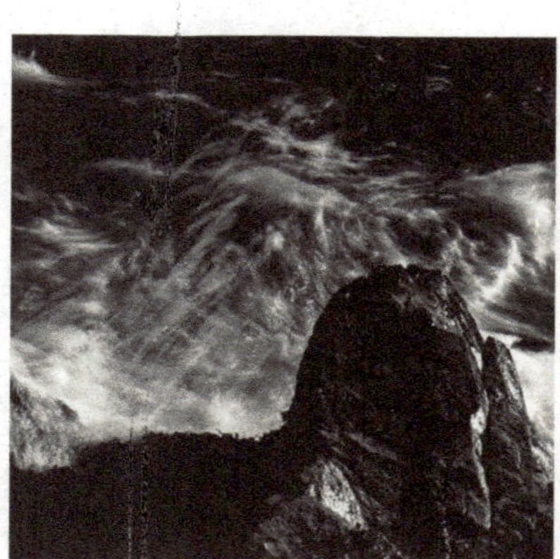
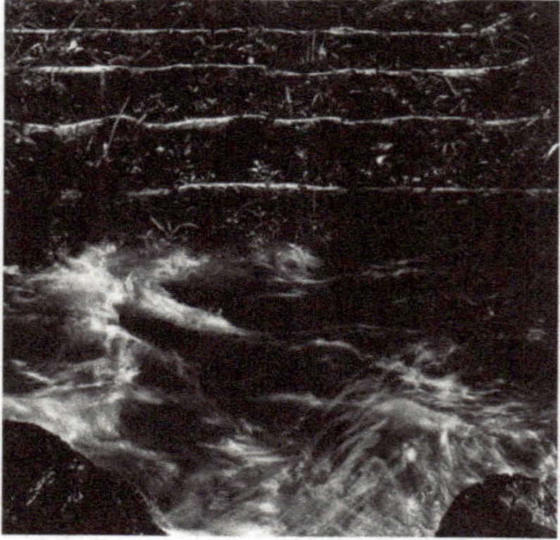

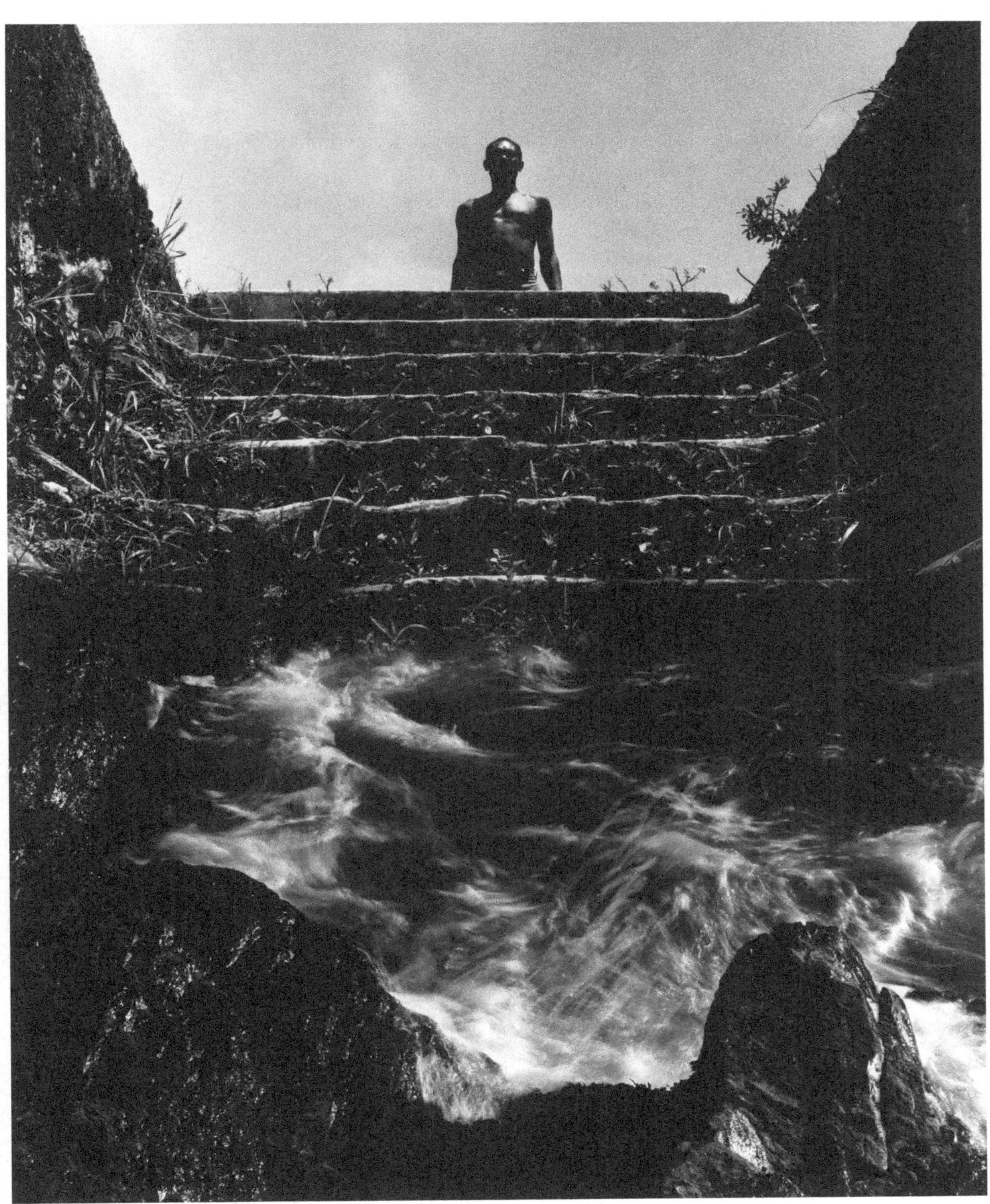

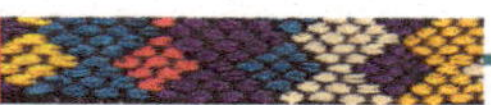

But I can say the oppression was so widespread and went on,
On and on in early 30s Alabama, the trial
And the convictions gone all the way up to the Supreme Court
Only to be reversed, and sent back as if it would change things
Swirling with more and more fury. But I really didn't see
Any of that back then as a child.   I just learned it later.
I could see only my loving parents. There's no substitute
For the start that they can give you: images and the feeling
Carried until your last day."

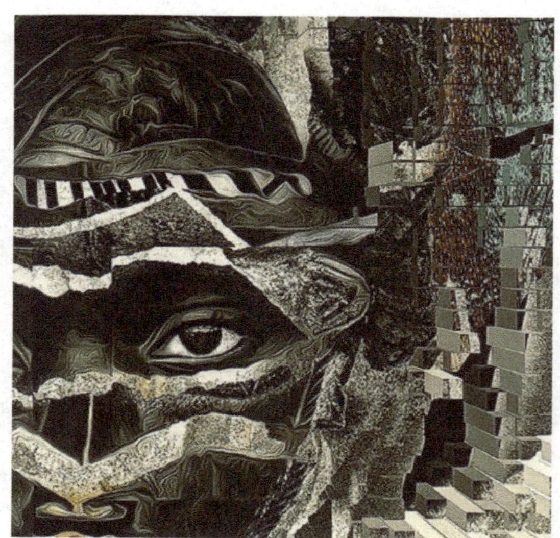

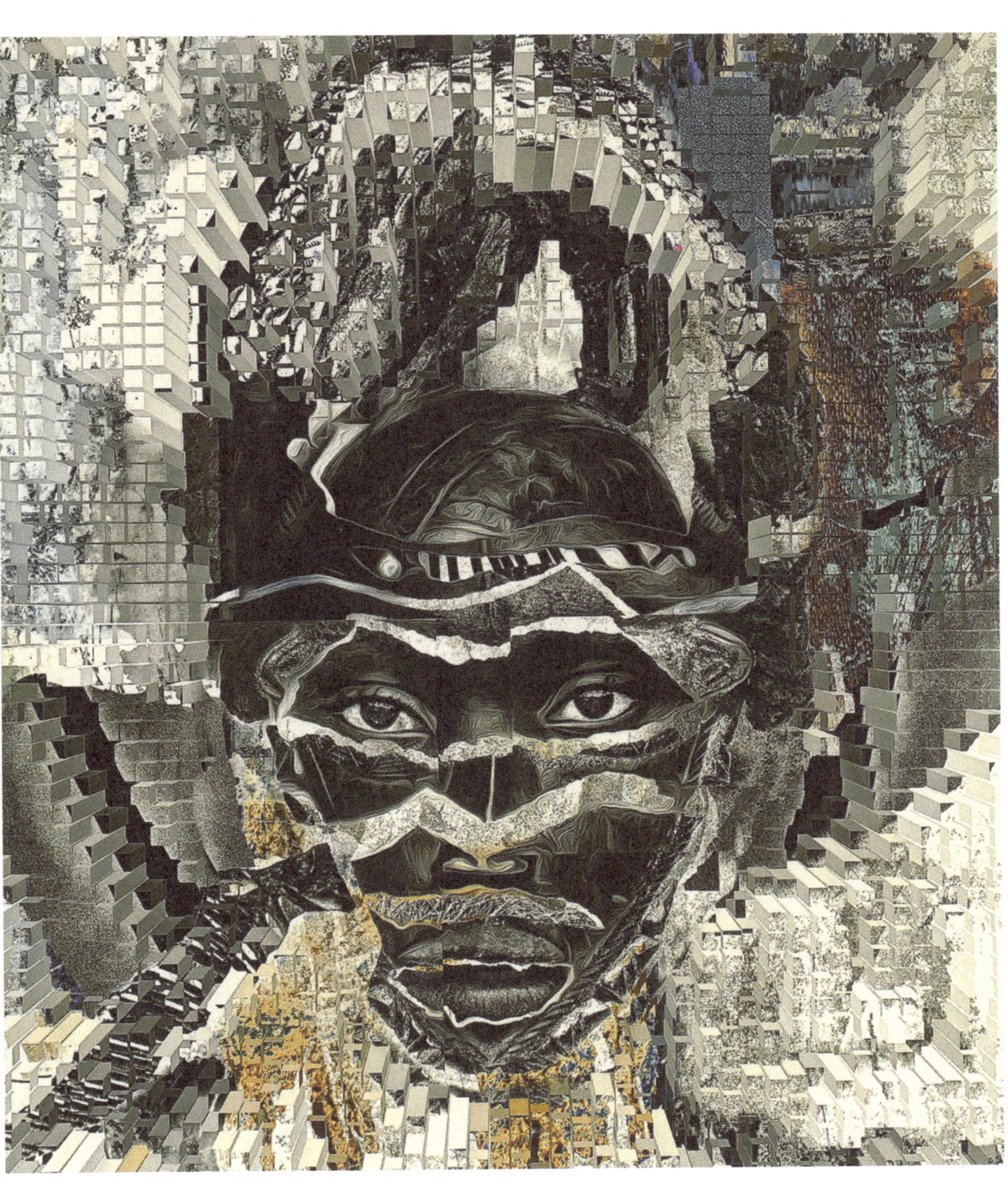

As if the dictum that "for now we see through a glass darkly"
Wouldn't apply to these frames and what was really there or not.

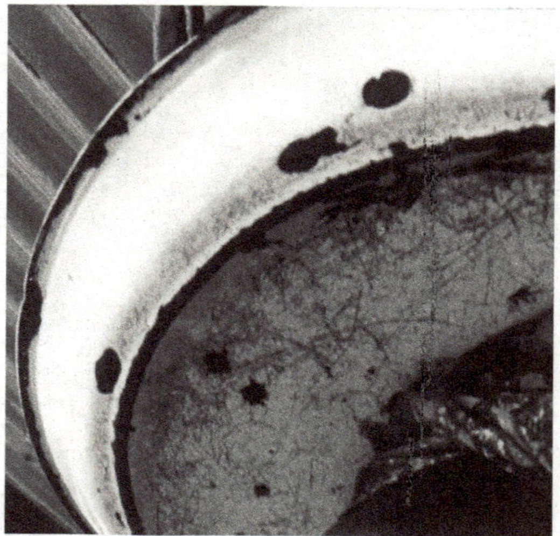

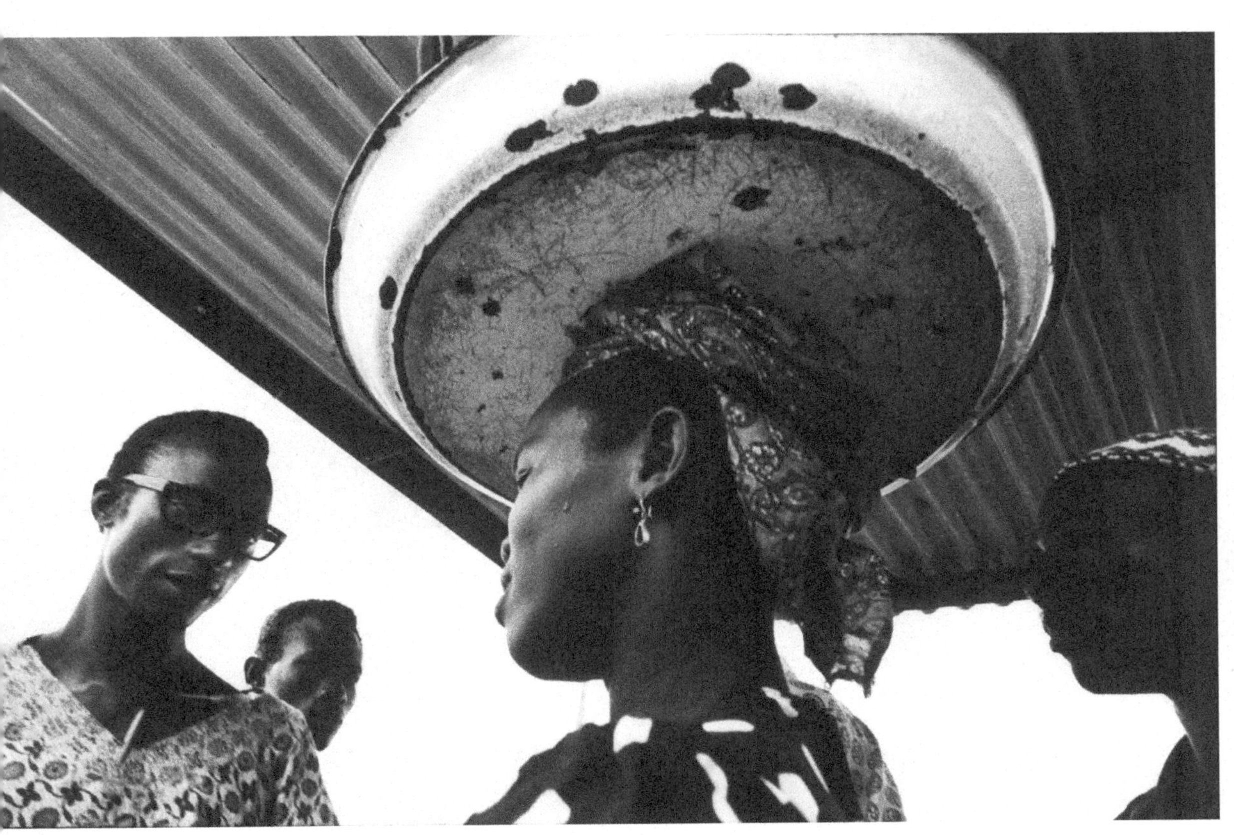

Meanwhile the window invited looking out on the landscape,
Hazy and lush blue and green instead of visual clichés
Merely to illustrate mundane walls of regimental rote:
Leaving no doubt about who's in charge and getting the message….

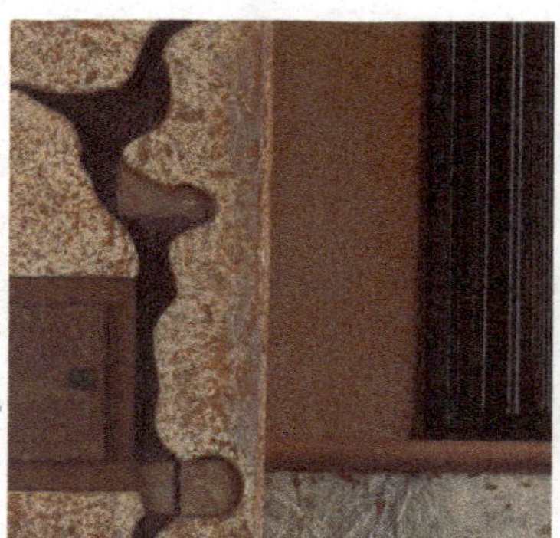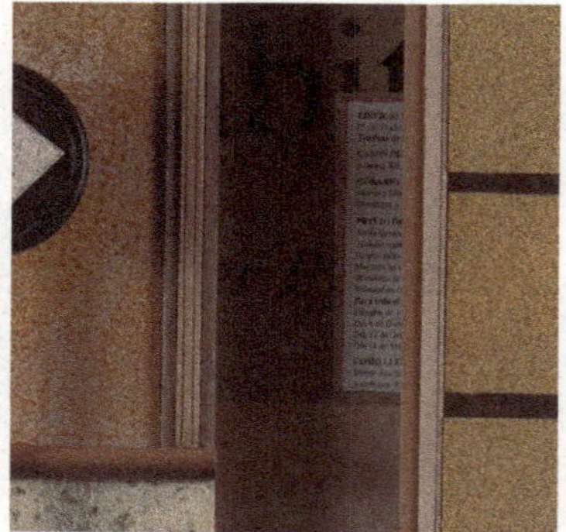

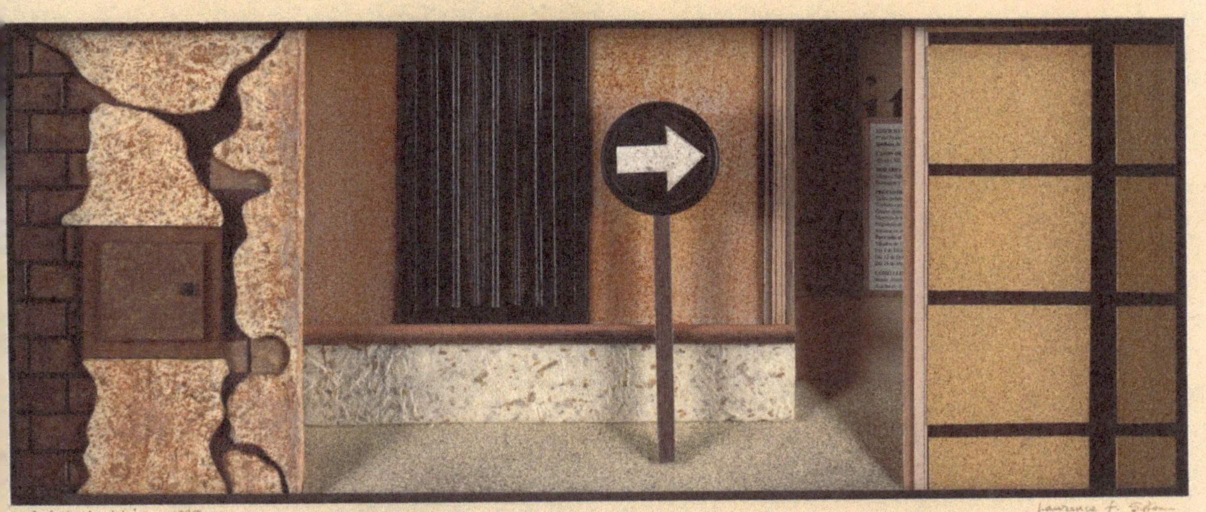
Ôséñlla Variñtiön, 1945

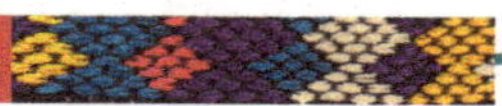

Sykes always guided me on the path I couldn't see alone.
As did his father decide to leave behind like my grandpa
One kind of history burning so another kind could be

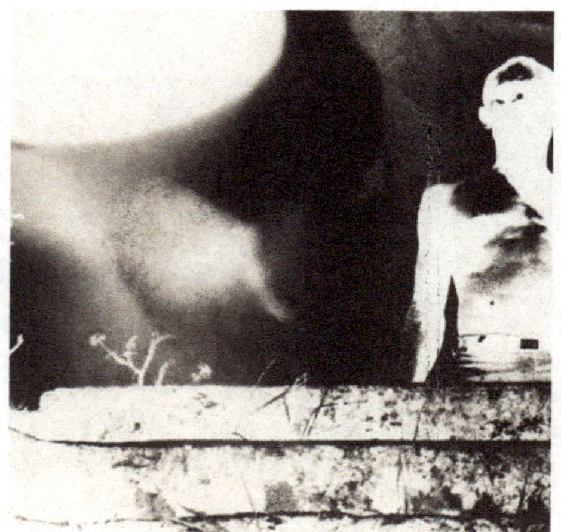

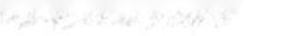

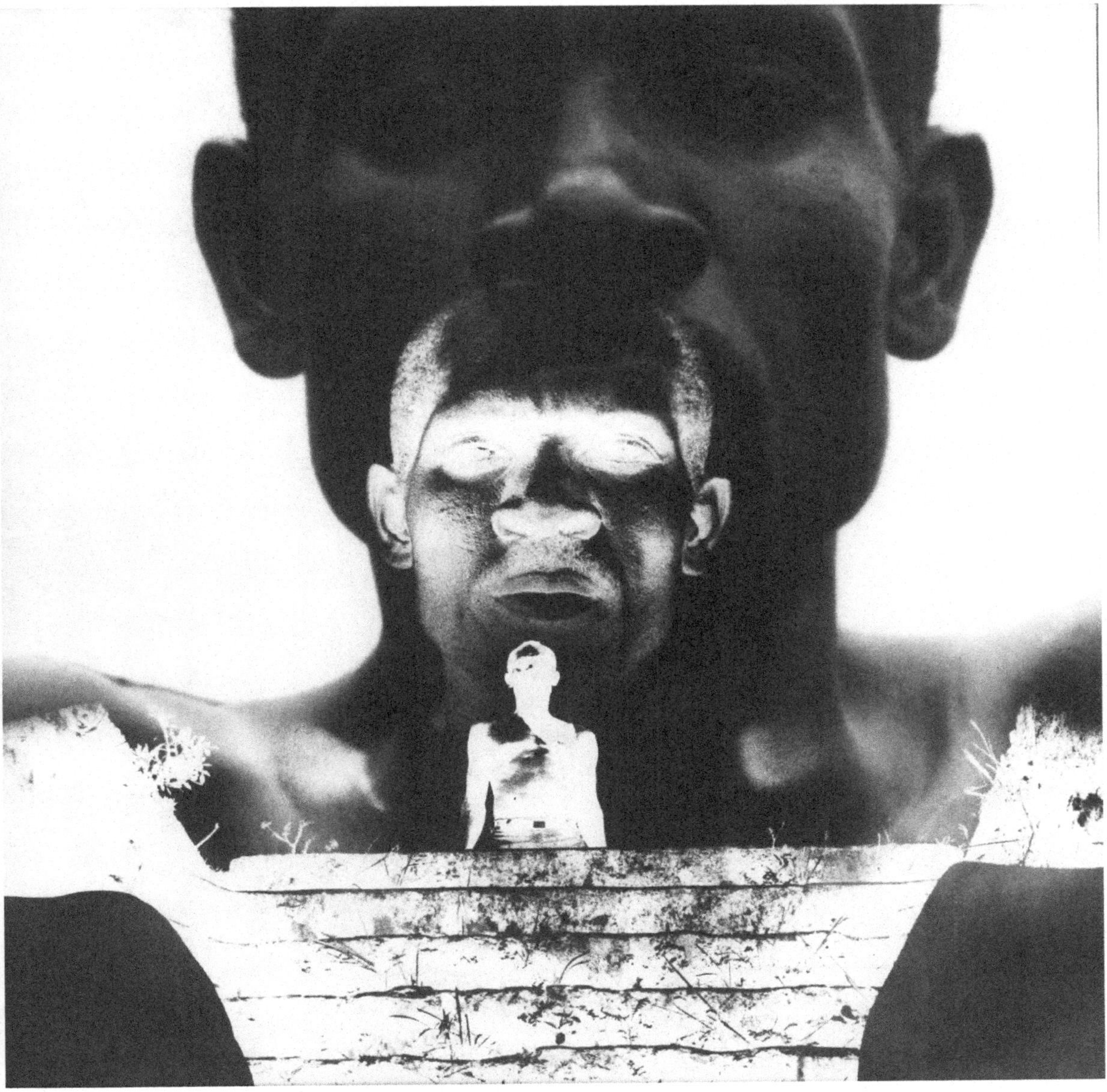

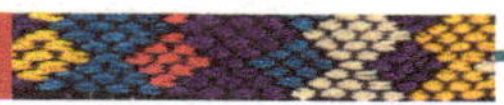

Taking the pictures unseen until they happened, even when
He alone saw them and showed us they were always happening.
Thus, people every day in a doorway could be there or not,
As could a tank from the war, a celebration, passersby,
Landscape or cityscape, empty courtyard – who knows when or why:
Really or conjured by Sykes yet absolute....

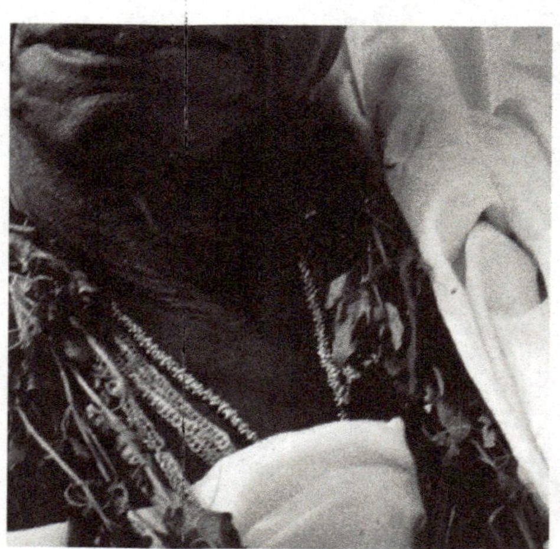

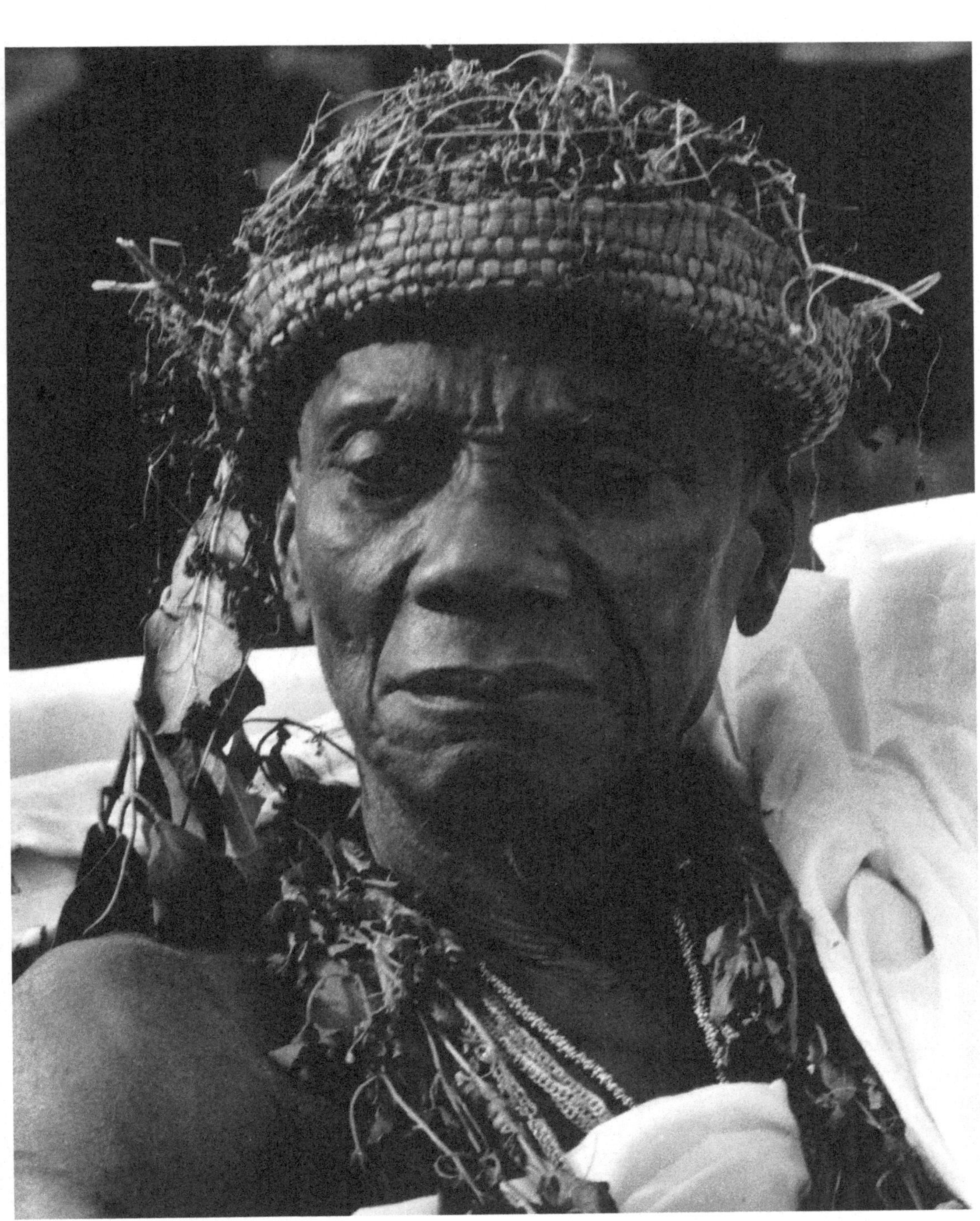

"During the second world war a friend took me to a pawn shop,
And with the money that I had saved I bought a camera."

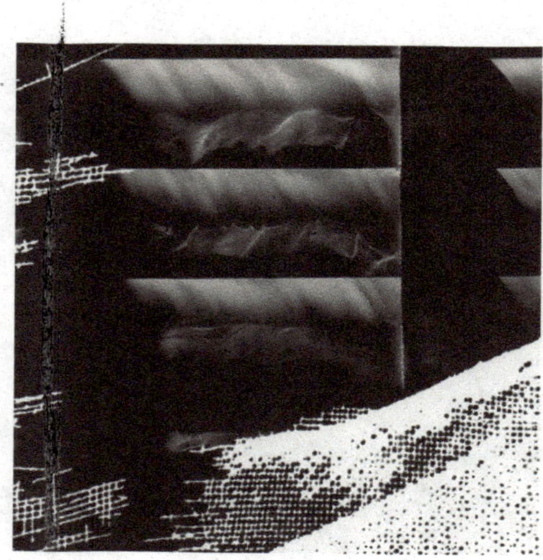

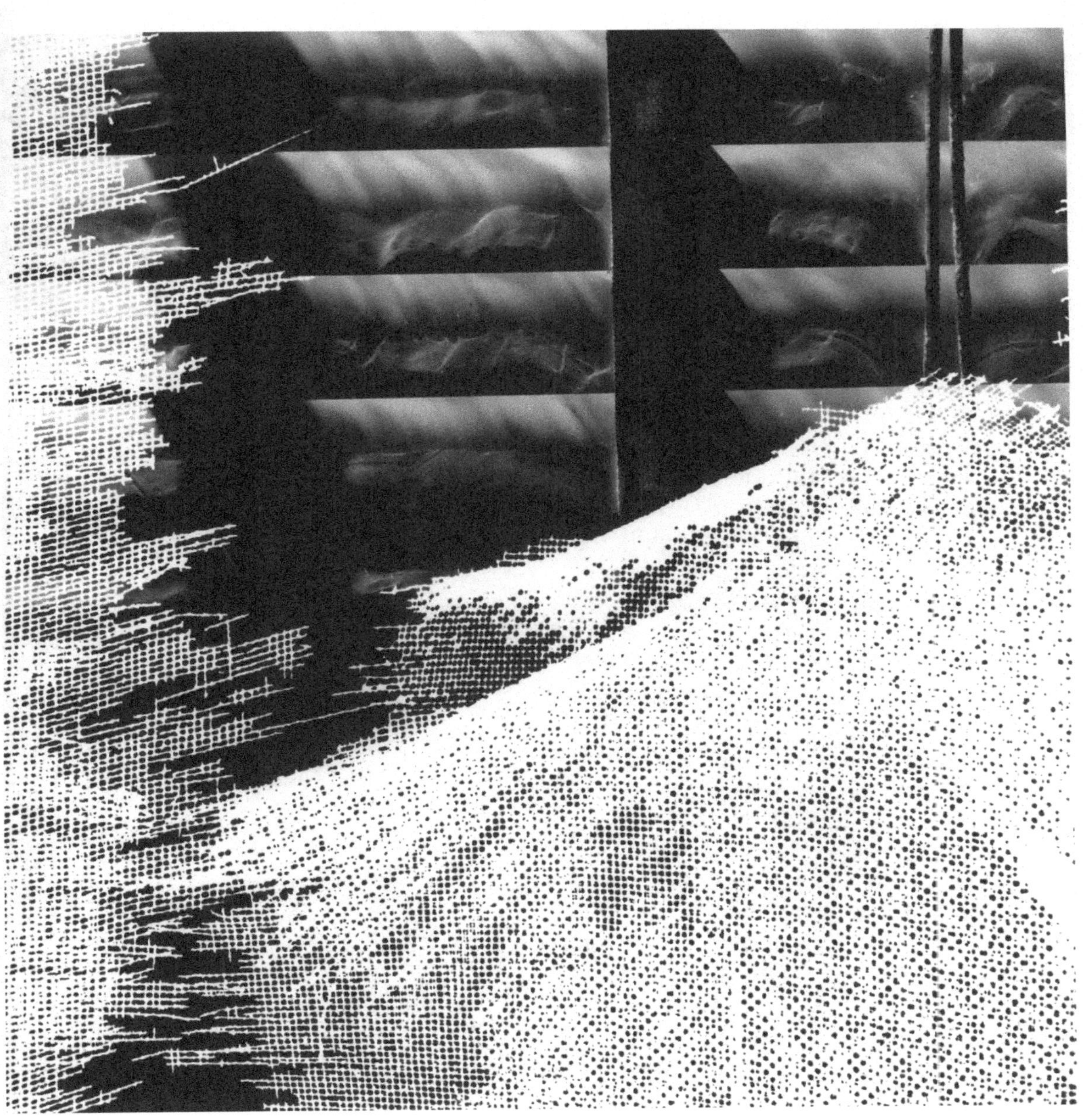

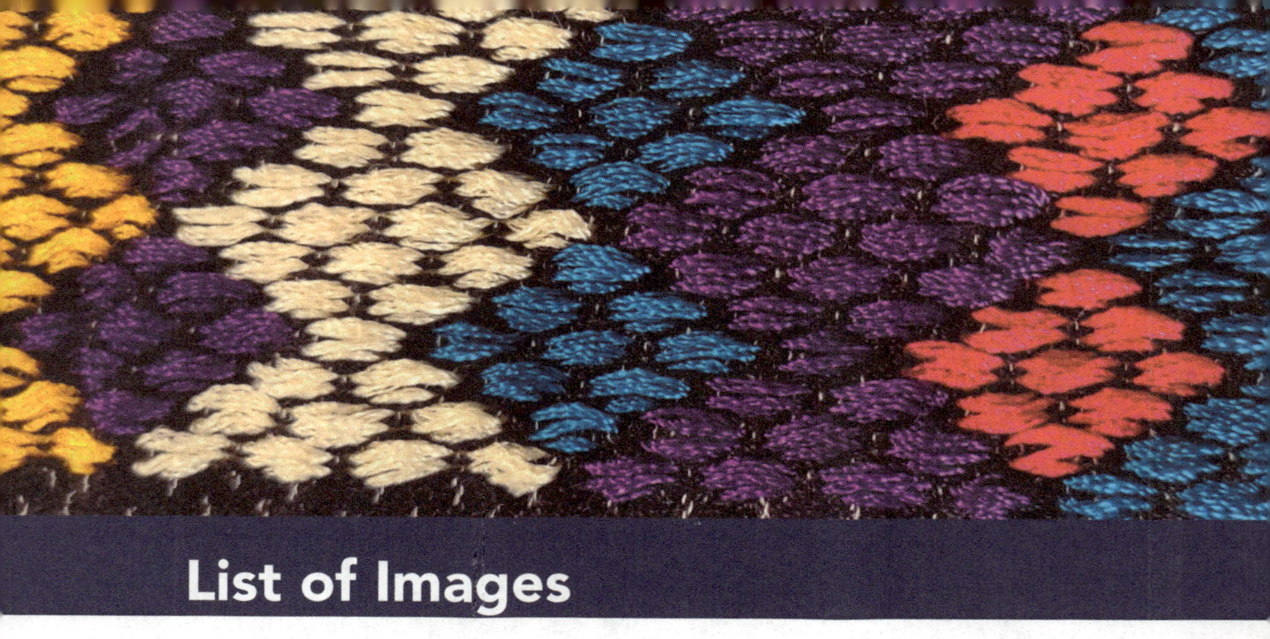

List of Images

Asmara, 1998, pp. 3,6,7,9,11,13, 15, 17, 19, 21, 23
Massawa, 1998, pp. 25, 27, 28, 29, 31, 33-54
"Set Shot," 1981, Boston, pp. 56 (detail), 57
Gorée Island, pp. 58 (detail), 59
Conjurgraph, Haiti, pp. 60 (detail), 61
Boston, pp.62 (detail), 63
Conjurgraph, pp. 64 (detail), 65
Asantehene, Kumasi, 1972, pp. 66 (detail), 67
Triptych, Boston, pp. 68 (detail), 69
Dockside, Ghana, 1972, pp. 70 (detail), 71
Diptych, pp. 72 (detail), 73
Conjugraph, Florence, pp.74 (detail), 75
Conjurgraph, pp. 76 (detail), 77
Haiti, pp. 78 (detail), 79
Conjurgraph, pp. 80 (detail), 81
Conjurgraph, pp. 82 (detail), 83
Mask, pp. 84 (detail), 85
Ferry Vendor, Ghana, 1972, pp. 86 (detail), 87
Seville, pp. 88 (detail), 89
Antoine Rising, pp. 90, (detail), 91
Kumasi, pp. 92 (detail), 93
Conjurgraph, pp. 94 (detail), 95

Acknowledgements

Collecting and sharing the work of Lawrence F. Sykes (1931-2020) have many sources of inspiration and support. His art brings them together, making possible the publication of *Sykes in Eritrea*. As he put his family first, so should *Sykes in Eritrea* first say thanks to them: Barbara J . Sykes; Kirk and Tammy Sykes; Kyle and Sydney Sykes; Zoe, Denny, and Sommer Heyman; Charles and Ania Sykes; Alice Sykes; Kim, Ric, and Mira Markink, and Susan Perez Gratitude also extends to friends: Joseph Norman, Berge Ara Zobian, and Angelo Marinosci. Thanks to Nichole Shea, Statewide Metadata Coordinator, and Bhahdir Kavlakli, Boston Public Library; and Tom Scott, (formerly of BPL). Gratefully acknowledged are Edmund Barry Gaither, Director and Curator of the Museum of the National Center of Afro-American Artists, and Special Consultant at the Museum of Fine Arts; Makeeba McCreary, Patti and Jonathan Kraft Chief of Learning and Community Engagement, Museum of Fine Arts; Kate Chertavian Lucy Rosenburgh, Kate Chertavian Fine Art; Sandy and Paul Edgerley, The 'Quin House. Penn State Lehigh Valley and Z Gallery are thankfully acknowledged, as are Mkuki na Nyota Publishers, Hdri Publishers, and *Warscapes* for previous publication of images from *Sykes in Eritrea*. Thanks to the Red Sea Press: the publisher, Kassahun Checole, and the production team, Dawid Kahts and N'Bsrat. Barbara Cantalupo – thank you for seeing and recreating Sykes in "detail" and, as always, for close editing.

Immense gratitude to Charles Cantalupo, whose "brainchild" is this book. Charles and Dad shared a special bond around Eritrea. They experienced the land through one another's eyes and souls. It is hard to imagine how these images and words could happen without one another. To Charles and his decades of friendship with Dad and our families, we owe a tremendous debt of gratitude. Most people leave this earth without a mark. Sykes and Cantalupo have left their mark on this world with this celebration of their love of Eritrea and art.

Kirk A. Sykes

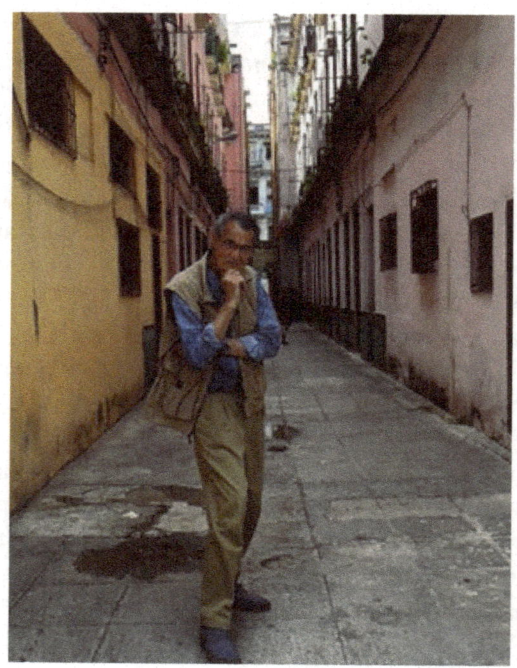

Lawrence F. Sykes, Cuba, 2016